HEAT WAVE!

The Best of *Chile Pepper* Magazine

Books by Dave DeWitt and Nancy Gerlach

The Fiery Cuisines

Fiery Appetizers

The Whole Chile Pepper Book

Just North of the Border

The Habanero Cookbook

by Dave DeWitt

Hot Spots

Chile Peppers: A Selected Bibliography of the Capsicums

by Dave DeWitt and Paul Bosland

The Pepper Garden

by Dave DeWitt and Arthur Pais

A World of Curries

by Dave DeWitt and Mary Jane Wilan

The Food Lover's Handbook to the Southwest

Callaloo, Calypso, and Carnival: The Cuisines of Trinidad and Tobago

by Dave DeWitt, Mary Jane Wilan, and Jeanette DeAnda

Meltdown: The Official Fiery Foods Show Cookbook and Chilehead Resource Guide

by Dave DeWitt, Mary Jane Wilan, and Melissa T. Stock

Hot & Spicy & Meatless

Hot & Spicy Chili

Hot & Spicy Latin Dishes

HEAT WAVE!

The Best of *Chile Pepper* Magazine

200 GREAT RECIPES FROM HOT & SPICY WORLD CUISINES

edited by Dave DeWitt and Nancy Gerlach

THE CROSSING PRESS
FREEDOM, CA

Acknowledgments

First, we'd like to thank Robert Spiegel for making possible the existence of a magazine devoted to chiles and spicy world cuisine. We also appreciate the invaluable efforts of the rest of the magazine's creative team, Lois Bergthold and Melissa Stock. Our contributing editors have greatly helped us to shape the magazine, so a tip of the hat to Sharon Hudgins, Richard Sterling, and Robb Walsh. And, *muchas gracias* to all of our writers, too numerous to mention here but valued contributors to *Chile Pepper's* success over the years. We have credited recipes by our writers in the appropriate recipe introductions. Finally, thanks to all our loyal subscribers over the years—they are the ones ultimately responsible for the magazine's success.

Portions of this book originally appeared in *Chile Pepper* Magazine.
Used by permission.

Library of Congress Cataloging-in-Publication Data

DeWitt, Dave.
   Heat wave! : the best of Chile Pepper magazine : 200 great recipes from hot and spicy world cuisines
/ Dave DeWitt & Nancy Gerlach.
     p. cm.
   Includes index
   ISBN 0-89594-759-5 (paper)
   1. Cookery (Hot peppers) 2. Hot peppers. I. Gerlach, Nancy. II. Chile Pepper.
III. Title.
TX803.P46D482 1995
641.6'384--dc 20
                                                           95-24301
                                                               CIP

Contents

Introduction

For years, readers have urged us to publish a collection of the best recipes that have appeared in the pages of *Chile Pepper* magazine, and finally we are able to comply. But everyone should know that this is just a sampling of more than a thousand recipes published in the first forty issues of *Chile Pepper*. We call it "the best of" but it well could be the first of more volumes to come.

One of the most interesting aspects of this collection is the fact that it exists in the first place, for it owes its existence to a fluke of publishing and a leap of faith.

A Brief History of the Pepper Periodical

After authoring two early books on hot and spicy foods (*The Fiery Cuisines,* 1984, and *Fiery Appetizers,* 1985), we were looking for a way to continue our study of chile peppers and the foods prepared with them. Through a mutual friend, we learned that an Albuquerque publisher, Robert Spiegel, was looking for new projects. We approached him with the idea for an annual publication that would serve the chile pepper industry. We would provide the editorial material, and Robert would sell advertising and arrange for distribution. The publication would be called—in a punning reference to the '60s—*The Whole Chile Pepper Catalog.*

We attempted to cram as much information as we could on chiles into a 48-page publication, including botany, identification, gardening, sources, cooking, and even a Chile Aficionado's Final Exam. Advertisers responded well to the idea, and we had full-page color ads from Joy Canning (now Basic American Foods) of Las Cruces and Fiesta Canning of Phoenix, both green chile producers. *The Whole Chile Pepper Catalog,* with a small print run of 10,000, hit the newsstands in the summer of 1987.

Although we called it a catalog, it looked like a magazine, and people assumed that there would be subsequent issues. We had not done much planning beyond making the first issue a success and thus had not inserted a subscription offer in it. But that didn't stop the chileheads, and we received two blank checks for subscriptions. "Just fill in the amount," wrote one trusting soul, "and send more magazines about chiles."

The national publicity we received on *The Whole Chile Pepper Catalog* was nothing short of astounding. Local stories were picked up by national wire services and soon our publication—and phone number—appeared in hundreds of newspapers across the country. The response was overwhelming and led to the inescapable conclusion: the public wanted a chile pepper magazine.

Robert made the decision to launch as a semiannual publication, with two issues scheduled for 1988 and four for 1989. To attract subscribers, he did a mailing to all the names he had compiled from the publicity on the first issue. A total of 212 people subscribed at first. Well, it was a start. In order to fund the launching of a magazine, Robert borrowed every cent he could find, including cash advances on credit cards. It turned out to be a risk well worth taking.

We actually published three issues in 1988, Spring, Summer, and Fall. We dropped the word *Catalog* from the masthead, and we developed many of the departments in the magazine that exist to this day, covering such subjects as chile peppers in the diet, spicy seafood, and hot, spicy Asian cooking. We went quarterly in 1989, but in 1990 had grown sufficiently to go bimonthly. In mid-1990, we shortened our name to just *Chile Pepper*. During this time, publicity remained strong as other publications were amazed that there was a magazine devoted to a "narrow niche" like chile peppers. That niche proved to be far larger than anyone—even us—imagined.

Our subscription base continued to increase and we also expanded to national newsstands, particularly those in large bookstores. We gained three contributing editors, Sharon Hudgins, Richard Sterling, and Robb Walsh, who helped us develop our theme, "Spicy World Cuisine," by covering the hot and spicy scene in Europe, Southeast Asia, and Mexico. We also were able to hire a full-time art director, Lois Bergthold, who developed the present masthead and magazine design.

Over the years, our subscribers grew from 212 to more than 35,000, with total circulation approaching 75,000 and a total readership per issue of more than 200,000. These may seem like large numbers, but compared to other food magazines, we are one of the smaller ones. Most magazines grow by spending vast sums of money on direct mail campaigns for new subscribers, but we have never had the capital for that. Instead, we have grown by word of mouth and reader loyalty.

Additional milestones for the magazine were the arrival of Melissa Stock as assistant editor (and eventually managing editor) and the publication of our fortieth issue in March/April, 1995. It, like our very first issue, had an article on gardening and extensive coverage of exotic chile cuisines.

In forty issues, we have circled the globe many times in search of hot and spicy foods, and we present some of the finest examples of what we've discovered in the recipes that follow. Accompanying the recipes are chile pepper anecdotes that appeared in the Hot Flashes department of the magazine. Additionally, we have included a reading list of our favorite hot and spicy books, and mail-order sources for exotic ingredients.

About the Recipes

The recipes come from our correspondents, writers, featured chefs, contest winners, and, of course, our own staff. Because of the international nature of our selections, some exotic ingredients are needed. Such ingredients are often found in specialty food stores, gourmet sections of supermarkets, and Asian and Latin markets. Many are available by mail-order. Our readers have told us that, over the years, exotic ingredients have become much easier to find.

We have tried to be specific as to the variety of chiles needed in the recipes and to suggest substitutions for the particularly unusual varieties. In most cases, substitute like for like. For example, if the recipe calls for fresh jalapeños, substitute another small, hot green chile such as serrano. If the recipe calls for dried piquins, substitute any small, hot red chile.

We have included a heat scale for each recipe, with the levels rated at mild, medium, hot, and extremely hot. These ratings take into consideration the variety of chile, the amount of it in the recipe, and the degree to which it is diluted with other ingredients. However, the ratings are only approximate and are not a substitute for the cook's own tasting.

Dousing that Burning Mouth

It just doesn't make any sense to serve or consume dishes that are simply too hot to eat. Of course, the definition of "too hot to eat" depends upon the taster, but if you have a hunch before you begin or discover later that your recipe is too blistering, here are some ways to cool it down:

- Reduce the amount of chile in the recipe to begin with. You can always add more heat later.
- Remove the seeds and membranes (placental tissue) from the chile pods.
- Increase the amount of tomato products—if any—used in the recipe, like tomato sauce, purée, or whole tomatoes.
- In appropriate recipes, like enchiladas, add a side of sour cream.
- If using canned chiles, rinse them well to remove the canning liquid.
- If making a sauce calling for green chiles, add puréed bell peppers to dilute the heat.
- When buying crushed red chile, avoid products with yellow flakes, which indicate the presence of seeds and membrane.

Now, if you or one of your fellow diners is literally burned out, here are some suggestions to cool down the mouth and throat:

- The best solution is immediate consumption of dairy products such as sour cream or ice cream.
- Starchy foods like bread or potatoes tend to absorb capsaicin. In New Mexico, we use sopapillas with honey.
- Various cultures have their own cures. The Chinese use white rice, the Vietnamese suggest hot liquids like tea, and the Indians (from India) utilize yogurt-based drinks and sauces.
- A Mexican cure calls for beer because if you drink enough of it, you won't care how spicy the food is.

The Heat Scales

The heat scale for each recipe is indicated by a graphic of a hot sauce bottle, according to the following ratings:

= no heat (desserts)

= mild

= medium

= hot

= extremely hot

Drinks for Spicy Foods and Eye-Opening Appetizers

Agua Fresca

Anyone who has traveled in Mexico has seen these refreshing fruit drinks in large glass jars being sold on street corners. We've used watermelon but almost any fruit can be used. Just adjust the amount of sugar depending on how sweet the fruit is and decrease the amount of lime juice if the fruit is acidic. These juices will keep, under refrigeration, for 4 to 5 days.

- **3 cups watermelon, chopped**
- **4 tablespoons sugar**
- **3 tablespoons lime juice, fresh preferred**
- **1 quart of water**
- **Watermelon chunks for garnish**

Place the watermelon, sugar, and lime juice in a blender or food processor and puree until smooth. Add the puree to the water and mix. Strain into a pitcher and discard any pulp.

Add the melon chunks just before serving.

 Yield: 1 quart

Mango Lassi

This refreshing drink originated in India, where it is often served for dessert after a meal of fiery hot curries. Other fruits may be added to or substituted for the mango.

- **2 cups plain yogurt**
- **2 cups buttermilk, or substitute milk**
- **Meat of two ripe mangos**
- **Juice of 1 lemon**
- **1 teaspoon sugar**

Place all ingredients in a blender and process until smooth. Serve over ice or freeze until slushy and then serve.

 Serves: 4

Hot New Mexican Chocolate

This recipe is an adaptation of traditional Mexican chocolate, which is made with melted Mexican bar chocolate—a combination of sugar, cinnamon, and cloves. Traditionally the hot chocolate is beaten at the table with a molinillo, a special carved wooden stirrer. It's lots of fun and adds a bit of showmanship. These stirrers are available in Mexican specialty shops.

- **1/3 cup cocoa**
- **1 tablespoon flour**
- **1/3 cup sugar**
- **3/4 teaspoon ground cinnamon**
- **1/4 teaspoon ground cloves**
- **1 cup water**
- **1 pint half & half**
- **1 cup milk**
- **1 1/2 teaspoons vanilla**
- **1 cup whipped cream**
- **Freshly grated nutmeg**
- **6 whole cinnamon sticks**

Combine the cocoa, flour, sugar, cinnamon, and cloves with the water in a saucepan. Stir or whisk until well blended and heat until it just barely begins to simmer.

Gradually add the half & half, and then the milk in a fine stream, stirring constantly. Add the vanilla. Beat with a molinillo, whisk, or rotary beater, and heat until hot, but not boiling. Keep warm for at least five minutes.

Just before serving, whip the chocolate again until it is frothy. Pour into mugs, top with a dollop of whipped cream, a pinch of nutmeg, and serve with a cinnamon stick.

 Serves: 6

New Mexico Roadrunner

Try this Southwest version of an old standby on a hot summer day.

- 1 ounce pepper vodka
- 1/2 ounce Amaretto
- 1/2 ounce coconut cream
- 1/4 cup crushed ice
- Sliced lime

Place all the ingredients except the lime in a blender and puree until smooth. Pour into a glass, garnish with a lime slice, and serve.

 Serves: 1

Pepper Vodka

- 4 jalapeños, stems removed, sliced in half, seeds removed
- 1 quart vodka

Place the chiles in the vodka and let sit for a couple of weeks or more. The longer the chiles are left in, the hotter the vodka. Remove the chiles when desired heat level is achieved.

 Yield: 1 quart

Captain John's Rum Punch

Sipping on a tall glass of fruited rum and watching the sun settle into the Caribbean sea are quintessential vacation memories for many island visitors. Fortunately, without even traveling to the West Indies, you can experience the very best rum drink ever served: just mix up a pitcher of this punch. For the glorious sunsets, you are on your own. This recipe was collected by Peggy Barnes.

- 3 cups passion fruit juice
- 1 cup guava juice
- 1 cup pineapple juice
- 2 cups orange juice
- 1/2 cup light rum
- 1/2 cup dark rum
- Several shakes of Angostura bitters
- 2 tablespoons aged dark rum (Appleton's 12-year-old from Jamaica is our favorite)
- Freshly grated nutmeg

Combine all the ingredients, except the aged rum and nutmeg, in a large pitcher and stir well to blend. Pour over ice in tall glasses.

Float the aged rum on top, garnish with the nutmeg, and serve.

 Yield: 2 quarts

Singapore Sling

This is a version of the famous drink as served in Penang, Malaysia. The major ingredients are two kinds of gin and two kinds of brandy.

- 2 tablespoons sloe gin
- 1 tablespoon dry gin
- 1 tablespoon apricot brandy
- 1 tablespoon cherry brandy
- 1 teaspoon sugar
- Juice of 1/2 lime
- Ice cubes
- Seltzer water
- Cherry for garnish
- Slice pineapple for garnish
- Slice orange for garnish

Combine the sloe gin, dry gin, apricot brandy, cherry brandy, sugar, and lime juice in a 12-ounce glass and stir well to dissolve the sugar. Add ice cubes and top off with seltzer water. Stir slightly, add the garnishes, and serve.

Serves: 1

Since the authors began their research on chile peppers in 1975, they have maintained a list of the maladies supposedly treated or cured by the use of either locally applied or ingested chile peppers. The list continues to grow because of newly-discovered historic citations and recent scientific and medical studies. Only those maladies marked with an asterisk (*) have demonstrated any firm medical basis for the efficacy of chile peppers.

Acid indigestion, alcoholism, anorexia, apoplexy, arteriosclerosis, arthritis, *asthma, *blood clots, boils, bronchitis, cancer, catarrh, childbirth, colic, colds, *congestion, coughs, cramps, croup, dropsy, dysentery, ear infections, epilepsy, fever, gout, herpes, liver congestion, malaria, migraine, night blindness, *phantom limb pain, rheumatism, seasickness, *scurvy, sore throats, stomachache, tonsillitis, toothache, tumors, ulcers, vascular problems, venereal disease, vertigo, wounds.

Curiously, chile is also reputed to aggravate some of the very conditions it's supposed to relieve: acid indigestion, cancer, dysentery, ulcers, and wounds.

Francisco "Pancho" Morales's Perfect, Original Margarita

Collected in Juarez by Elaine Corn, this purportedly is the drink invented by Pancho Morales. Use hunks (not cubes) of ice and never use shaved ice. The formula requires enough tequila (please, a great tequila like Herradura) and Cointreau (never Triple Sec), two parts to one, to equal exactly 4 ounces of drink. "This takes some skill," warns Corn, "but it's not brain surgery."

"The two parts doesn't mean jigger and it doesn't mean bottles," advises Pancho.

Juice of 1/2 Mexican (Key) lime
Salt
2 parts white tequila
1 part Cointreau

Squeeze about an ounce of lime juice into a bartender's glass filled with ice chunks. Take the squeezed lime and run it around the rim of a 4-ounce cocktail glass. Sprinkle the rim lightly with salt and shake off all the excess. Allowing for the juice already in the bartender's glass and any ice that may have melted to contribute to the 4-ounce final tally of liquid, add the tequila and Cointreau to equal 4 ounces. Cover the bartender's glass. Shake, strain, and pour into the cocktail glass.

 Serves: 1

Fire God Frozen Margarita

Here is a newfangled version of the margarita, prepared with a spicy tequila.

1 1/2 cups Fire God Tequila or any spicy tequila
8 fresh Mexican (Key) limes, or enough to make 1/2 cup juice
1/3 cup Triple Sec
2 cups crushed ice
Salt
Sliced lime

Prepare 4 long-stemmed goblets by rubbing the rims with a piece of lime; dip the rims in salt and place in the freezer for at least 30 minutes.

Pour the tequila, Triple Sec, and lime juice in a blender, add the ice until the blender is half-full and then process. Taste the result and adjust the flavors by adding more Triple Sec to make it sweeter, more lime juice to make it more tart, more tequila to increase the heat level, or more ice to decrease the heat level.

Pour into the frosted goblets and garnish with a slice of lime.

 Serves: 4

"Buffalo News" Buffalo Wings

Serve the wings on a platter garnished with celery sticks and blue cheese dipping sauce. Accompany with beer, wine, or soft drinks. This recipe is from contributor Howard Shatz.

1 egg
1 cup vegetable oil
1/4 cup ground cayenne
2 cups cider vinegar
1/2 teaspoon freshly ground black pepper
1/4 teaspoon onion powder
1/4 teaspoon garlic powder
1/4 teaspoon ground nutmeg
1/8 teaspoon celery salt
1/8 teaspoon ground coriander
1/8 teaspoon ground cloves
2 pounds chicken wings
Celery sticks
Buffalo Blue Cheese Dressing

Prepare the sauce by beating the egg and the oil together. Add the other ingredients, except the last three ingredients, and mix well.

Remove the tips from the chicken wings and separate each wing at the joint. Rinse and dry each wing section. Dip the wings in the hot sauce and place in a shallow roasting pan.

Broil until done, about 10 to 15 minutes, brushing the wings with the sauce and turning them occasionally.

Yield: 20 to 24 wings

BUFFALO BLUE CHEESE DRESSING

1 cup mayonnaise
1/2 cup sour cream
1/4 cup crumbled blue cheese
1/4 cup finely chopped parsley
2 tablespoons finely chopped onion
1 tablespoon lemon juice
1 tablespoon white vinegar
1 teaspoon minced garlic

Combine all ingredients and chill for 1 hour before serving.

Yield: 1 3/4 cups

Tsingtao Beer, brewed in the People's Republic of China, has a new slogan: "Chinese Fire Extinguisher"— an obvious reference to the fiery cuisines of Sichuan and Hunan provinces.

Rocoto Relleno
(Andean-Style Stuffed Hot Chiles)

Rocoto peppers are not available in the United States but any hot chiles, large enough to be stuffed, can be substituted, although they may not have the rocoto's true fiery effect.

> 12 to 16 rocotos, or substitute large
> jalapeños or yellow wax chiles
> 1/2 pound ground beef
> 1 medium onion, diced
> 1 clove garlic, crushed
> 1/3 cup raisins
> 2 hard-cooked eggs, chopped
> 8 black olives, sliced
> 4 slices bread, soaked in milk then
> squeezed and drained
> 2 ounces grated gouda cheese

Preheat the oven to 350 degrees.

Carefully cut the stems out of each chile and remove the seeds through the hole at the top.

Brown the ground beef along with the onion and garlic. Remove from the heat and mix in the raisins, eggs, olives, bread, and cheese.

Through the hole in the top of the chiles, stuff them with the mixture. Close the whole with a plug of cheese. Place the filled chiles in a casserole dish, cover, and bake for 20 minutes.

 Serves: 4

Ceviche with Ajis

There are many ceviche dishes throughout Latin America, but the original recipe for this tasty appetizer is credited to Peru. The acid in the juice "cooks" the fish.

> 4 aji chiles or 4 serrano chiles, stems
> and seeds removed, cut in strips
> 1 pound firm white fish, such as snapper,
> pompano, flounder, or bass, cut into
> 1 1/2-inch cubes
> 1 small purple onion, thinly sliced and
> separated into rings
> 1 cup bitter orange juice
> 1 large sweet potato, cooked, peeled and sliced
> 2 ears corn, cooked and cut in half
> Lettuce

Place the chiles, fish, and onion in a nonreactive bowl; cover with the orange juice and refrigerate for 2 to 4 hours, turning occasionally until the fish loses its translucency and turns opaque. To serve, drain the fish and arrange it and the onion on a bed of lettuce. Place a sweet potato slice on one side and a corn portion on the opposite side. If you use whole kernel corn instead of the ears of corn, put it with the fish to marinate or add the kernels later after the fish is "done."

 Serves: 4

Note: This recipe requires advance preparation.

BITTER ORANGE JUICE

> 1/2 cup grapefruit juice
> 1/4 cup orange juice
> 3 tablespoons lime juice

Mix all the juices together and use within 24 hours.
Yield: 3/4 cup

Ceviche de Palapa Adriana— Acapulquito Style

If you wish to try Acapulquito Style ceviche at Palapa Adriana, a restaurant on the Malecon in La Paz, Baja California Sur, you must specially request it. The ceviche which is listed on the menu will be served without the peas, carrots, and serrano chiles. This dish can be served as a light lunch.

1 1/2 pounds of any firm white fish, such as snapper, pompano, flounder, or bass, cut into 1 1/2-inch cubes

Juice of 8 Mexican (Key) limes

2 serrano chiles, stems and seeds removed, minced

6 to 8 small corn tortillas

Vegetable oil for frying

1 medium tomato, finely chopped

1/2 medium onion, finely chopped

1/4 cup cooked peas

1/4 cup finely diced carrots

2 teaspoons minced cilantro

Salt and freshly ground black pepper to taste

Place the fish and chiles in a nonreactive bowl; cover with the lime juice and refrigerate for 2 to 4 hours, turning occasionally until the fish loses its translucency and turns opaque.

Pour the oil to a depth of an inch, heat it, and quickly fry the tortillas for a few seconds until they are crisp. Remove and drain on paper towels. Reserve these.

Just before serving, stir the vegetables and the cilantro into the marinated fish and chiles. Add salt and pepper to taste. With a slotted spoon, heap the ceviche onto the crisp tortillas and serve.

Serving Suggestions: If tostaditas are available in your area, they may be used in place of the crisply fried tortillas.

Variation: Use tiny cocktail shrimp or sliced bay scallops in place of the fish. Reduce the marinating time to 30 minutes or less.

 Serves: 6 to 8

The late John Riley, former editor-publisher of the quarterly journal *Solanaceae*, tested various folk remedies reputed to remove the heat of the capsaicin in chile peppers. In each test, a slice of serrano chile was chewed for one minute, and then one of the remedies was applied. The amount of time until the burning sensation eased was measured and the results were recorded. Ordinary milk was the clear winner.

Spring Rolls

These crispy little rolls are popular appetizers. They resemble Chinese egg rolls, but are much more delicate. Handling rice paper for the wrapping is easier than it looks. Use only a couple of sheets at a time and keep the rest covered with a damp towel to stay moist. Use a high-grade vegetable oil for the frying. The rolls can be cooked and frozen. Thaw and reheat in a 350 degree F oven.

2 ounces cellophane noodles

6 dried Chinese mushrooms

8 ounces raw shrimp, shelled
 and deveined

1 pound ground pork, cooked

2 eggs, beaten

3 serrano chiles, stems and seeds
 removed, minced

1/2 small jicama, shredded

1 small carrot, shredded

1 small onion, minced

3 green onions, shredded

3 cloves garlic, minced

2 tablespoons Nuoc Nam
 (Vietnamese fish sauce)

40 small rounds rice paper
 (6-inch diameter)

Vegetable oil for frying

Nuoc Cham Sauce

Soak the cellophane noodles in warm water for 20 minutes. Drain and cut into 1-inch lengths.

Soak the Chinese mushrooms in warm water for 20 minutes and drain. Remove the stems and finely mince.

Roughly chop the shrimp. Combine the pork, noodles, mushrooms, and shrimp with the eggs, chiles, jicama, carrot, onion, garlic, and fish sauce.

Fill a shallow dish with warm water and immerse a round of rice paper for a few seconds to become pliable. Drain the rice paper and spread it out on a towel.

To assemble, fold up the bottom third of a rice paper, put a tablespoonful of filling on it, and shape the filling into a little rectangle. Fold the sides over the filling to form a roll.

Pour the oil into a skillet to a depth of 2 inches and heat to 325 degrees. Fry the rolls, a couple at a time, until golden.

Serve with Nuoc Cham Sauce for dipping.

 Yield: 36 to 40

Nuoc Cham Sauce

2 tablespoons fresh lime juice

2 tablespoons Nuoc Nam (Vietnamese
 Fish sauce)

4 dried red chiles, stems and seeds
 removed, such as piquin or Thai,
 or substitute 4 serrano chiles

1 clove garlic

2 teaspoons sugar

3 or more tablespoons water

Place all the ingredients in a blender or food processor and puree until smooth.

 Yield: 1/2 cup

Clams Pica-Pica

We first tried these clams in a small restaurant in Juarez, Mexico, and liked them so much that we included them in our book, Fiery Appetizers!

4 jalapeño chiles, stems and seeds removed, chopped

1 large tomato, peeled and chopped

1 small onion, minced

2 cloves garlic, minced

1 tablespoon lime juice

12 large clams in the shell

Garnish: Chopped cilantro, thinly sliced onion

Place the chiles, tomato, onion, garlic, and lime juice in a blender or food processor and puree until smooth.

Open the clams and discard the top shell, leaving the meat in the bottom of the shell. Place the clams in a shallow pan, meat side up. Place a small amount of the sauce on each clam and bake for 15 minutes.

Serve the clams with the chopped cilantro and sliced onion on a side platter and a frosty Mexican beer.

 Yield: 12

Hot and Cheesy Artichoke Dip

This dip can be prepared a day in advance and refrigerated. The next day bring the dish to room temperature, and then bake it. Serve in a chafing dish with crisp tortilla or corn chips.

3/4 cup chopped green New Mexico chiles

1 6-ounce jar marinated artichoke hearts, drained and chopped

1 8 1/2-ounce jar artichoke hearts, drained and chopped

1/4 cup mayonnaise

2 cups grated cheddar cheese

Preheat the oven to 350 degrees.

Combine the chiles and artichoke hearts and spread the mixture over the bottom of a greased, shallow baking dish. Spread the mayonnaise over the artichokes and top with the cheese.

Bake for 15 minutes or until the cheese melts and the dip is hot.

 Yield: 2 1/2 cups

Polish Baked Stuffed Mushrooms

Mushroom picking is a national pastime in Poland— mushrooms are an important ingredient in many Polish dishes. In the mountainous region of the south, mushrooms are often combined with locally made cheeses, as in the following recipe. The Poles would use fresh Boletus edulis *mushrooms and salty sheep's milk cheese known as bryndza—but large champignons and Greek feta are acceptable substitutes outside of Poland. This recipe was collected in Poland by contributing editor Sharon Hudgins.*

1 pound (16 large) champignon
  mushrooms

6 tablespoons melted butter or margarine

1 shallot, finely chopped

1 large clove garlic, minced

1 tablespoon finely chopped parsley

2 teaspoons mild or medium-hot paprika
  or to taste

1/2 cup dry bread crumbs

1/2 cup finely crumbled sheep cheese
  such as feta

Preheat the oven to 350 degrees.

Carefully twist the stems off the mushrooms, leaving the cap whole, and finely chop the stems.

Heat half the butter, add the chopped stems, shallot, and garlic, and saute for about 5 minutes. Remove the pan from the heat and stir in the parsley, paprika, and bread crumbs. Add the crumbled cheese and mix well.

Lightly brush the outside of each mushroom cap with the remaining butter. Stuff each cap with a heaping tablespoon of the filling, shaping the filling by hand into a small dome. Use all of the filling to stuff the 16 mushroom caps. Arrange the mushrooms, filling side up, in a lightly oiled baking dish. Bake for 15 to 20 minutes.

Serve hot as a first course or as an accompaniment to broiled steaks or chops.

 Yield: 16 mushrooms

Thirteen shoppers were hospitalized and the Fallbrook Mall in California's San Fernando Valley was evacuated when an irritating cloud of smoke filled the mall on March 17, 1987. Firefighters searching for the source of the fire finally uncovered the culprit: the blackened remains of cayenne chiles in a frying pan.

It seems that a cook at one of the specialty food restaurants in the mall accidentally burned the peppers while cooking them in hot oil and caused considerable panic. Since the smoke from burning hot chiles was once used as a chemical warfare weapon in pre-Columbian South America, cooks should always exercise caution when sauteing chiles in oil.

Nelly's Empanadas

Empanadas, meat-filled turnovers, are very popular throughout Latin America where they are most often eaten as a snack. This recipe was collected in Argentina by Susan Hazen-Hammond.

Crust:
  1 2/3 cups all-purpose flour
  1/8 teaspoon salt
  4-ounce stick butter or margarine
  1/3 cup milk
Filling:
  1 pound ground beef
  1 to 2 tablespoons vegetable oil,
    olive preferred
  1 large onion, finely chopped
  1 red bell pepper, stem and seeds
    removed, finely chopped
  2 jalapeño chiles, stem and seeds
    removed, minced
  1 medium potato, peeled, boiled,
    finely chopped
  2 hard-cooked eggs, finely chopped
  10 to 12 green olives, finely chopped
  2 tablespoons raisins
  1 tablespoon ground mild paprika
  1 tablespoon chopped parsley
  Salt and freshly ground black
    pepper to taste
Glaze:
  1 egg, beaten
  1 tablespoon milk

To make the crust, sift the dry ingredients into a bowl. Work the margarine or butter into the flour using your fingers or two forks. Add the milk and mix just until the dough comes together and can be formed easily into a ball. Refrigerate for at least an hour.

Saute the beef in oil in a skillet until well done, stirring frequently with a fork to keep the meat broken up. Drain off any excess fat.

In a separate skillet, saute the onion, bell pepper, and jalapeños in the oil until the onions are a golden brown. Combine all the ingredients for the filling and mix well.

Preheat oven to 400 degrees.

Divide the dough in two and roll out to a thickness of 1/8 inch and cut into circles 7 inches in diameter. Spoon the filling onto one-half of each, leaving room to fold in half and seal. Press the edges with the tip of a fork and cut a 1-inch slice in the top. Place on an ungreased baking pan.

Combine the ingredients for the glaze.

Bake for 10 minutes. Reduce the heat to 350 degrees and continue baking until the crust turns light brown. Brush the tops with glaze and bake for an additional 5 minutes.

 Yield: 10

Fresh Maine Crabcakes with Jalapeño Aioli

Steve Cobble of the Green Street Grill in Cambridge, Massachusetts, serves these crabcakes as an appetizer, but they are tasty enough to be an entree as well. The aioli sauce should be slightly sweet, chunky, and yellow, with a smoky heat that creeps up on you.

2 eggs, slightly beaten

3/4 cup sour cream

2 teaspoons Dijon mustard

Juice of 1 lemon

Juice of 1 lime

2 green onions, thinly sliced

2 fresh cayenne chiles or 3 jalapeños, stems removed and minced

1 teaspoon cracked ground black pepper

1 teaspoon allspice berries, cracked

2 teaspoons salt

1 pound crabmeat

2 cups bread crumbs, from day-old bread

Vegetable oil for frying, peanut preferred

Jalapeño Aioli

Combine the eggs, sour cream, mustard, lemon and lime juices, green onions, chiles, black pepper, allspice, and salt, and mix thoroughly. Gently fold in the crabmeat and then the bread crumbs. Form into patties 1/2-inch thick.

Pour the oil into a skillet to a depth of 2 inches and heat. Pan fry the patties until brown on both sides.

Serve the crabmeat cakes with the Jalapeño Aioli on the side.

 Serves: 4

JALAPEÑO AIOLI

1 teaspoon achiote paste or substitute 2 teaspoons ground annatto*

2 cups vegetable oil, canola preferred, divided

2 egg yolks

2 teaspoons minced garlic

1 teaspoon Dijon mustard

1 teaspoon honey

Juice of 1 lemon

Juice of 1 lime

2 jalapeño chiles, roasted but not peeled, sliced into rings

1 cup fresh pineapple, finely diced

1/2 cup chopped cilantro

2 teaspoons pineapple juice

Salt and freshly ground black pepper to taste

Crush the achiote paste into a saucepan and add 1/2 cup of the oil. Heat until almost boiling, remove from the heat, and cool to room temperature.

Place the egg yolks, garlic, mustard, and honey in a food processor or blender. While the machine is running, slowly drizzle in the remaining 1 1/2 cups of oil, alternating with the lemon and lime juice. Add the achiote mixture last. Transfer to a bowl and fold in the remaining ingredients.

 Yield: 2 1/2 cups

*Available in Latin markets or through mail order.

Serbian Lamb and Beef Sausage Rolls

In Serbia, these delicious meat rolls are cooked over fires of grape branches.

- 1 small onion, chopped
- 1/2 teaspoon minced garlic
- 1 tablespoon vegetable oil
- 1 pound ground beef
- 1 pound ground lamb
- 1 egg white, lightly beaten
- Salt to taste
- 1 tablespoon Hungarian paprika
- 3 tablespoons finely minced onion
  for garnish

Garnish: Hot pickled chiles, cut into rings

Saute the chopped onion and garlic in oil until they are translucent and remove them to a bowl. Add the beef, lamb, egg white, salt, and paprika and mix well. Pinch off pieces of the mixture and form into 1- by 2-inch rolls or elongated meatballs. Cover the meat and refrigerate for several hours.

Prepare a barbecue grill and when the coals are white, thread the meat rolls onto skewers leaving a little space between them. Grill over charcoal for up to 10 minutes on each side, until meat rolls are done in the center.

Remove the rolls from the skewers and sprinkle with minced onion. Arrange them on a serving dish and garnish with the chile rings and serve.

Serves: 6

A unique culinary taste-test was once conducted at the Coyote Cafe in Santa Fe, New Mexico. Under the direction of chef/owner Mark Miller, ten California wineries gave tastings of their Sauvignon Blancs in combination with red and green chile dishes created by chef Miller. The object was to see how the wines held up against the heat and flavor of the various chiles.

The menu included such delicacies as Fresh Gulf Crab Cushions with Dried Green Chile and Tomatillo Sauce, Squash Blossoms Stuffed with Local Wild Mushrooms with Roasted Green Chile Sauce, Roasted Corn and Fresh Herb Tamale with Chile Pasado Sauce, and Pecan-Grilled Fresh Sea Scallops with Painted Plate of Red Chile and Vanilla Crema.

We valiantly devoured every course of the experimental dinner and left the restaurant convinced that Sauvignon Blancs are indeed an excellent complement to chile dishes. These wines do not dominate the spicy flavors as beers have a tendency to do. However, once the chile began to burn the palate slightly, it was more difficult to distinguish between the two wines being served with each course.

Sate Kambing (Skewered Lamb)

Here is a tasty appetizer from Indonesia, where kabobs are called sates. *In addition to being marinated and basted with chiles, the* sates *are often served with a hot chile paste called a* sambal *or the Indonesian Peanut-Chile Sauce (page 34).*

1 medium onion, coarsely chopped

1 clove garlic, minced

3 tablespoons ketjap manis (Indonesian sweet soy sauce)

1 tablespoon lime juice, fresh preferred

1 teaspoon ground ginger

1 teaspoon ground coriander

1 tablespoon ground cayenne

1 tablespoon olive oil

2 pounds of leg of lamb or lamb shoulder, cut in 1-inch cubes

2 jalapeño chiles, stems and seeds removed, minced

24 8-inch bamboo skewers, soaked in water

Combine the onion, garlic, soy sauce, lime juice, ginger, coriander, cayenne, and olive oil to form a marinade. Marinate the lamb overnight, or at least 3 hours, in the sauce. Remove the meat and save the marinade.

Thread the lamb onto the skewers, putting about half-a-dozen on each. Leave a 2- or 3-inch handle at one end and pack the meat cubes closely together.

Prepare a charcoal grill and when the coals are hot, grill for 5 to 10 minutes, or under the broiler 2 to 3 inches from the heat source until the desired doneness.

Add the jalapeños to the reserved marinade and let this warm on the grill or stove while the sates cook. Turn the sticks methodically every couple of minutes until the meat browns evenly all around. Baste with the sauce.

Pour the remaining sauce over the grilled sates before serving.

Yield: 2 dozen

Note: This recipe requires advance preparation.

A demographics magazine once suggested that a part of Texas be separated and the new state be named Jalapeño.

Curry Puffs

Invented by the colonial British, these pastries are a favorite teatime snack in Singapore and Malaysia. They also make a fabulous appetizer!

- 1 package frozen prepared puff pastry
- 2 tablespoons vegetable oil
- 1 medium onion, finely chopped
- 2 tablespoons finely chopped ginger
- 2 tablespoons curry powder
- 8 ounces minced chicken or beef
- 3 to 4 serrano chiles, stems removed, finely chopped
- 1 medium tomato, chopped
- 1/2 teaspoon salt
- 1 large potato, peeled, boiled, and finely diced
- 2 tablespoons milk
- 1 egg, lightly beaten with 1 tablespoon milk

Preheat the oven to 425 degrees.

Allow the puff pastry to thaw to room temperature.

Heat the oil in a wok and stir-fry the onion and ginger for a minute, or until softened. Mix the curry powder with enough water to make a paste and add to the onion. Stir-fry for an additional minute. Add the meat and continue frying until the meat browns. Add the chiles and tomato, and sprinkle with salt.

Cover the pan and simmer for 10 minutes, stirring occasionally. Add water, a tablespoon at a time, if the mixture becomes dry. Add the potato and cook for another minute or so. Cool.

Roll out the pastry to about 1/8 inch thick and cut into circles, 3 1/2 inches in diameter. Brush the edges with milk, add a tablespoon of the curry filling, fold the edges closed and crimp decoratively with a fork. Brush the pastries with the egg-milk wash.

Bake on an ungreased cookie sheet for 12 to 15 minutes or until the curry puffs are golden brown and puffed. Serve warm.

 Serves: 4 to 6

Drinks for Spicy Foods and Eye-Opening Appetizers

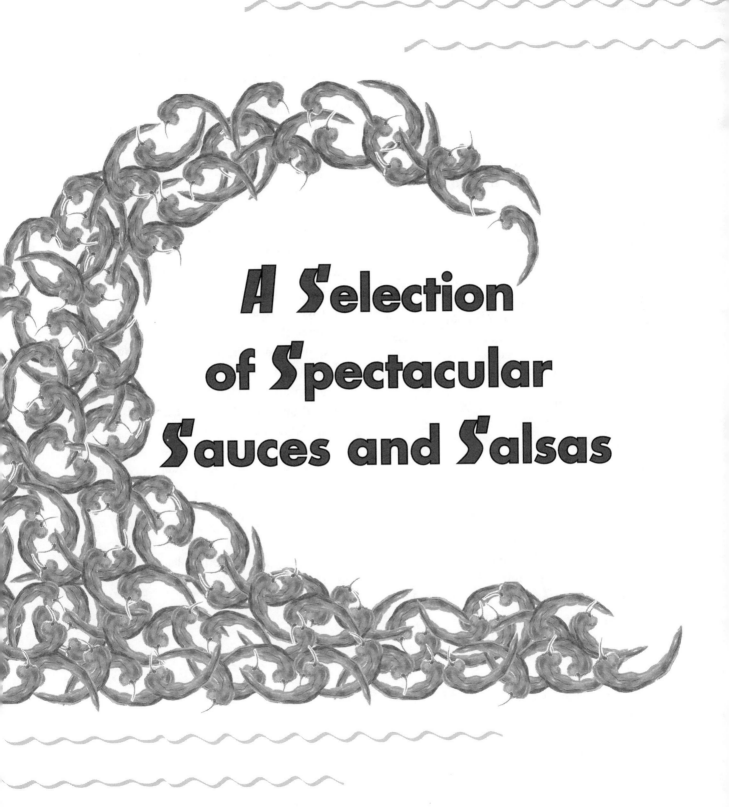

A Selection
of Spectacular
Sauces and Salsas

Salsa Yucateca de Habaneros

Below is the classic habanero salsa of the Yucatan, from Arturo Lomeli's cookbook, El Chile y Otros Picantes. *It is served with fish or other seafood.*

1 purple onion, finely chopped
1/3 head purple cabbage, finely chopped
2 habanero chiles, green preferred, stems and seeds removed, minced
2 radishes, finely chopped
Juice of 2 Mexican (Key) limes
2 tablespoons water
Salt to taste

Place the onion in a colander under a stream of water for a few seconds, drain. Combine with the cabbage, chiles, and radishes. Mix the lime juice and water together and add salt to taste. Pour over the vegetables and gently toss.

 Yield: 2 to 3 cups

Mango Salsa

Here the luscious flavor of mango is wonderful with the searing Scotch bonnet. Serve with anything grilled.

1 ripe mango, peeled and diced
1/4 cup minced purple onion
1 Scotch bonnet or habanero chile, stem and seeds removed, minced
2 tablespoons lime juice, fresh preferred
1 tablespoon minced cilantro
1/4 teaspoon ground cumin
1/4 teaspoon white pepper
1/4 teaspoon salt

Combine all of the ingredients in a bowl and mix thoroughly. Refrigerate for 1 hour before serving.

 Yield: 2 cups

Salsa Cruda de Chihuahua (Uncooked Salsa from Chihuahua)

Here is a traditional salsa from northern Mexico. Although the avocado is optional, it adds a great deal to the sauce. If you wish the salsa to be very hot don't seed the chiles.

1/4 cup chopped serrano chiles
1/4 cup chopped jalapeño chiles
1/4 cup chopped poblano chiles
1/4 cup chopped onion
2 tablespoons chopped green onions
1/2 cup lime juice
1/4 teaspoon salt
2 tomatoes, chopped
1 tomato, roasted, peeled, and blended until smooth
1/4 cup minced cilantro
1 medium avocado, peeled, seeded, and chopped (optional)

Place the chiles, onion, green onion, lime juice, and salt in a nonreactive bowl, mix well and refrigerate for 1 to 2 hours to blend the flavors. Drain and discard the lime juice.

Add the chopped tomatoes and just enough of the pureed tomato to bind the mixture into a sauce. Salt to taste. Add the cilantro and avocado, and serve.

 Yield: 1 1/2 cups

A Selection of Spectacular Sauces and Salsas

Salsa de Chile de Arbol (Chile de Arbol Sauce)

From Jim Peyton, who has authored two books on the cooking of the border, comes this great sauce. He says: "This is one of the hottest sauces I have ever tried. It takes a confirmed chilehead to enjoy it." It is served over side dishes such as beans or rice, but can also be used on meats and in stews.

    12 to 14 chile de arbols
    2 tablespoons cider vinegar
    2 cloves garlic
    1/2 teaspoon dried oregano,
       Mexican preferred
    1/2 teaspoon salt
    1/4 teaspoon ground cumin
    1/2 cup water, divided

Toast the chiles by heating them in a heavy skillet or comal over low heat until they are fragrant but not burned. Remove the stems.

Place the chiles in a blender or food processor with 1/4 cup of the water and all the remaining ingredients and blend until smooth. Add the remaining water and blend again.

Strain the sauce into a bowl and serve.

Yield: 1/2 cup

Sunbelt Salsa Fresca

There are many variations of this basic salsa from the Southwest to the tip of South America. It is called a cold sauce because it isn't cooked. Make sure that all the ingredients are chopped very fine.

    6 serrano or jalapeño chiles, stems and
       seeds removed, minced
    1 large onion, either yellow or
       purple, minced
    2 medium tomatoes, chopped very fine
    2 bunches finely chopped cilantro
    1/4 cup vegetable oil
    1/4 cup, or less to taste, red wine vinegar

Mix all the ingredients together and let stand at room temperature for at least an hour.

Yield: 2 cups

Tomatillo Salsa

This simple but delicious salsa is from El Norteño restaurant in Albuquerque, one of our favorite haunts. Serve it with chips or grilled meats and poultry.

    5 serrano chiles, or more, stems and
       seeds removed, chopped
    1/2 pound fresh tomatillos, chopped
    1/2 cup chopped white onion
    1 tablespoon chopped cilantro
    1/4 teaspoon salt

Place all the ingredients in a blender or food processor and puree, adding just enough water to make a thick sauce.

Yield: 1 cup

Habanero Mango Salsa

This salsa is from Chiletos Taqueria in Santa Barbara. The owner, Alex, says it goes well with pork and swordfish tacos. He notes that it is usually the women who come back for seconds, not the men.

- 5 dried habanero chiles, stems removed
- 2 tablespoons chopped white onion
- 1 pound fresh mango, peeled and chopped, or frozen if fresh not available
- 3 tablespoons golden raisins
- 1/8 teaspoon ground turmeric
- 1 fresh lime, quartered

Cover the chiles with water in a saucepan. Add the onion and simmer until the chiles are softened. Add the mango and the raisins, raise the heat and, just before the mixture begins to boil, remove from the heat.

Place the chile mixture and turmeric in a blender and puree until smooth. As it is blending, squeeze the lime juice in the salsa, being careful not to breathe the fumes.

 Yield: 1 1/2 to 2 cups

Argentinian Chimichurri Salsa

This South American salsa is used as a relish It is served at the table and spread on charbroiled steaks.

- 6 cloves garlic, minced
- 4 tablespoons lemon juice, fresh preferred
- 2 tablespoons olive oil
- 1 tablespoon chopped parsley
- 1 teaspoon crushed red chile, such as New Mexican, piquin, or de arbol
- Salt and freshly ground black pepper to taste

Combine all the ingredients and place in a nonreactive container. Allow the salsa to sit in the refrigerator overnight. Remove 1 hour before using and stir well. Just before serving, stir again.

 Yield: 1/4 cup

Note: This recipe requires advance preparation.

Cilantro Chutney

Put a spoonful in soups or stews, use it as a dip for fresh vegetables, or dab it on grilled meat or poultry.

- 1 cup chopped cilantro stems and leaves
- 1/4 cup coconut milk
- 1/4 cup minced onion
- 1/4 cup lemon juice
- 1/4 cup cold water
- 2 tablespoons minced ginger
- 2 teaspoons Sambal Oelek*
- 1 teaspoon sugar
- 12 black peppercorns

Place all the ingredients in a blender or food processor and puree until smooth.

 Yield: 3/4 cup

*You can purchase Sambal Olek in Asian stores or through the mail.

Salsa de Pasilla

Although dried chiles are usually used in cooked sauces, this lusty, spicy salsa uses dried pasilla chiles to give an earthy taste that goes perfectly with marinated and grilled meats. Like most salsas, it is best made in a molcajete, or mortar, for the authentic, chunky texture—do not use a food processor. Serve on top of grilled meats or poultry.

6 dried pasilla chiles

2 tablespoons vegetable oil

2 serrano chiles, stems and seeds removed, minced

2 tablespoons minced garlic

1/2 cup chopped onion

Salt to taste

3 tomatoes, peeled and chopped

1 small, firm Haas avocado, diced

Pass the pasilla chiles over a gas flame until they are soft and pliable, taking care not to burn them. Remove the stems and seeds. Heat the oil slightly in a small saucepan. Place the pasillas in the pan, pressing down with a spatula until they heat up and barely begin to sizzle. Remove, blot with paper towels, and chop fine.

Place the pasillas, serranos, garlic, onion, and a little salt in a molcajete or nonreactive bowl and pound them into a rough paste. Add half the tomatoes and pound to a smooth paste. Add the remaining tomatoes and crush lightly. Stir in the avocado and adjust the seasoning.

 Yield: 1 to 1 1/2 cups

Peach Pecan Salsa

Central Texas is hill country, which produces both the pecans and peaches that are used in this recipe. An example of a new Southwestern style of cooking, this salsa is great with grilled chicken and fish.

1/2 cup sugar

1 cup orange juice

2 tablespoons vinegar

3 tablespoons crushed dried red New Mexican chile, including the seeds

1 stick cinnamon (2 1/2-inches)

1/4 teaspoon ground cumin

1 tablespoon finely grated orange peel

3 large peaches, peeled and chopped

1/2 cup toasted pecans, chopped

Dissolve the sugar in the orange juice and vinegar. Add the chile, cinnamon, cumin, and orange peel. Bring to a boil, reduce the heat, and simmer for 20 minutes until it becomes a thick syrup. Discard the cinnamon, add the peaches, and simmer for 5 minutes. Stir in the pecans and heat for an additional minute before serving.

Yield: 2 cups

Chile Pepper Water

Melissa Stock collected this unique Hawaiian sauce from Alan Wong, executive chef of Le Soleil at the Mauna Lani Bay Hotel and Bungalows. Alan says this recipe is hot, so use it sparingly. The chiles tend to settle at the bottom of the container in which you store the sauce. Therefore, before you use the sauce, be sure to shake the container to distribute the chiles evenly.

2 red jalapeño or serrano chiles, stems and seeds removed, cut in half
2 tablespoons minced ginger
1 tablespoon white vinegar
1/2 clove garlic
Pinch of salt
2 cups water, divided

Place the chiles, ginger, vinegar, garlic, and salt in a blender or food processor along with 1/3 cup of the water and puree until smooth.

Bring the remaining water to a boil, add the puree, and return the mixture to a boil.

Remove, cool, and place in a glass jar. This sauce will keep indefinitely in the refrigerator.

 Yield: 1 1/2 cups

Countryman's Boston Beach Jerk Sauce

Michael Baim collected this recipe from the Countryman restaurant at Boston Beach, Jamaica. Michael wrote us: "Countryman's jerk was flavorful and, because he doesn't remove the seeds or membrane from the chiles, hot. Rub this sauce into your favorite cut of pork or chicken, beef, or fish. The longer it marinates in the refrigerator (at least 4 hours, preferably overnight), the stronger the flavor. Chicken needs the longest time to marinate, fish the least. Slow cook over hardwood charcoal or use a gas grill with mesquite.

2 to 4 Scotch bonnet chiles, stems and seeds removed*
1 large mango or small papaya, peeled and chopped
1 medium onion, chopped
1/2 cup chopped green onions
2 teaspoons salt
2 teaspoons fresh thyme
1 teaspoon freshly ground black pepper
1 teaspoon ground allspice, Jamaican preferred
1/2 teaspoon ground cinnamon
1/4 teaspoon ground nutmeg

Place all the ingredients in a blender or food processor and process until they are roughly chopped.

 Yield: 1 1/2 cups

Variation: Soak 1/2 cup of raisins in rum overnight. Drain the liquid and add the raisins in place of the mango or papaya.

Note: This recipe requires advance preparation.

*If you wish to make a sauce as hot as Countryman's don't seed the chiles.

Chile Pepper Jamaican Jerk Marinade

The number of versions of jerk marinades are nothing less than astonishing. They range from the early, simple pastes of three or four ingredients to the more modern concoctions with as many as twenty-one ingredients. After careful taste-testing, we judged this marinade superb. By varying the amount of vegetable oil and lime juice, the cook can change the consistency from a paste to a sauce. It can be used with pork, chicken, or fish.

1/4 cup pimento berries (allspice berries), Jamaican preferred

3 Scotch bonnet chiles, stems and seeds removed, chopped

10 green onions, chopped

1/2 cup chopped onion

4 cloves garlic, chopped

4 bay leaves, crushed

2 tablespoons chopped ginger

1/3 cup fresh thyme leaves

1 teaspoon ground nutmeg

1 teaspoon ground cinnamon

1 teaspoon salt

1 tablespoon ground black pepper

1/4 cup vegetable oil

1/4 cup lime juice

Roast the pimento berries in a dry skillet until they are fragrant, about 2 minutes. Remove and crush them to a powder in a mortar or spice mill. Place all the ingredients in a blender or food processor and puree to make a sauce.

Store in the refrigerator; it will keep for a month or more.

 Yield: 2 to 3 cups

Basic Red Chile Sauce

This basic sauce can be used in a variety of Southwestern dishes that call for a red sauce, such as enchiladas. It can be used as well in place of catsup when making salad dressings and sauces.

10 to 12 dried red New Mexican chiles

1 large onion, chopped

3 cloves garlic, chopped

1 tablespoon vegetable oil

3 cups water or chicken broth

1/2 teaspoon dried oregano, Mexican preferred

Preheat the oven to 250 degrees.

Place the chiles on a baking pan and bake in the oven for 10 to 15 minutes or until the chiles smell like they are toasted, being careful not to let them burn. Remove the stems and seeds and crumble the pods into a saucepan. Set aside

Saute the onion and garlic in the oil until soft and add them to the chiles in the saucepan. Add the remaining ingredients, bring to a boil, reduce the heat, and simmer for 20 to 30 minutes or until the chiles are soft and the sauce has thickened.

Place the sauce in a blender or food processor and puree until smooth, then strain.

If the sauce is too thin, place it back on the stove and simmer until it is reduced to the desired consistency, and if it is too thick, thin with water or broth.

 Yield: 2 to 3 cups

A Selection of Spectacular Sauces and Salsas

Harissa Paste

This fiery pepper-paste is an essential ingredient in many couscous recipes. It is a flavoring agent and also a condiment. You can purchase good commercial harissa in small cans and tubes (like toothpaste), but the homemade version is easy to make and has an even better flavor. (Note: Some cookbooks recommend Indonesian sambal oelek as an acceptable substitute for harissa, but the flavor is actually quite different.) The following recipe is for the freshly made harissa paste that Sharon and Tom Hudgins first ate at a Tunisian restaurant in Paris. The waiter was shocked and pleased when they devoured the entire bowl . . . then asked for seconds . . . and finally asked for the recipe! Use this as a hot-spicy condiment to accompany couscous.

2 large pimientos, fresh, canned,
   or bottled, chopped
1/4 cup small hot dried red chiles, such
   as piquin, crushed
3 large cloves garlic, chopped
1 tablespoon finely chopped cilantro
1 teaspoon caraway seeds
1/2 teaspoon salt
1/4 teaspoon ground cumin
Olive oil

If using fresh pimientos, roast and peel them before using.

Combine all the ingredients, except the oil, in a blender or food processor and process until well blended. Transfer the paste to a glass jar and cover the top with 1/4 inch of olive oil. Keep the paste tightly covered and refrigerated until needed.

The harissa paste can be frozen.

Yield: 1/2 cup

Papaya Mustard Sauce

This recipe is from Caribbean food expert Jay Solomon. He wrote, "Papaya, also known as tree melon or pawpaw, has light-green to coral-yellow skin, with a pinkish-orange flesh. The sweet flavor of the fruit complements the floral heat of the Scotch bonnet. Serve this sauce with chicken, pork, or strongly flavored fish such as tuna, marlin, or mahi-mahi."

1 papaya, peeled and diced
1 tomato, peeled and diced
1/2 cup purple onion, diced
1 to 2 Scotch bonnet or habanero chiles,
   stems and seeds removed, minced
1/2 cup red wine vinegar
1/4 cup white wine
2 tablespoons Dijon-style mustard
2 tablespoons brown sugar
2 tablespoons Worcestershire sauce
1 teaspoon hot sauce, such as Tabasco
1/2 teaspoon ground allspice
1/4 teaspoon white pepper
1/4 teaspoon salt

Combine all the ingredients in a nonreactive saucepan and simmer, stirring occasionally, for 10 to 12 minutes or until the mixture has a jamlike consistency. Allow the sauce to cool to room temperature.

Place the mixture in a blender or food processor and process for 15 to 20 seconds. The sauce should be smooth with a few remaining chunks.

Serve immediately or refrigerate. The sauce will keep for about 2 weeks in the refrigerator.

Yield: 2 cups

Classic Mole Poblano

Here is the classic central Mexican chile sauce. It is used primarily with poultry and is particularly tasty served over smoked turkey breast. Enchiladas prepared with mole sauce and Mexican asadero *cheese (also called* queso blanco*) are as exotic as they are tasty. Optional ingredients or substitutions include anise, ground black pepper, tomatillos, pumpkin seeds, raw peanuts, plantains, cumin seeds.*

- 4 pasilla chiles, or substitute ancho, stems and seeds removed
- 4 dried red New Mexican chiles, stems and seeds removed
- 1 onion, chopped
- 2 cloves garlic, minced
- 2 medium tomatoes, peeled and chopped
- 2 tablespoons sesame seeds, divided
- 1/2 cup piñon (pine) nuts or almonds, finely chopped
- 1/2 corn tortilla, torn into pieces
- 1/4 cup raisins
- 1/4 teaspoon ground cloves
- 1/4 teaspoon ground cinnamon
- 1/4 teaspoon ground coriander
- 2 tablespoons vegetable oil
- 3 cups chicken broth
- 1 ounce bittersweet chocolate, or more to taste
- Salt to taste

Cover the chiles with hot water and let them sit for 15 minutes to soften. Remove the chiles and retain the water.

Combine the chiles, onion, garlic, tomatoes, 1 tablespoon of the sesame seeds, piñons, tortilla, raisins, cloves, cinnamon, and coriander. Puree small amounts of the mixture in a blender or food processor until smooth.

Heat the oil and saute the puree for 10 minutes, stirring frequently. Add the broth, 1/2 cup of the chile water, and the chocolate, and simmer the sauce for 30 minutes or until very thick. Add salt to taste.

Use the remaining sesame seeds to garnish the sauce when serving.

 Yield: 3 1/2 cups

Nicole Carroll told us, "Persistent pepper hounds can find chile pepper pasties with tiny swinging ristras, a matching garter with tiny red and green chiles...chile-shaped earrings, necklaces, bolo ties, switchplates, candles, windsocks, cutting boards, dinnerware, placemats, salsa dishes, crystal goblets, business card holders, door knockers, and drawer handles (each in the shape of a different chile). For the four-legged fan there are pepper-shaped chew toys and catnip pods."

Red Pipian Sauce

Mark Miller, an early star of Chile Pepper, *was featured in an article entitled "Chile Chefs from Coast to Coast." His excellent sauce is usually served over poultry or pork.*

- 2 dried ancho chiles, stems and
  seeds removed
- 4 dried guajillo chiles, or substitute New
  Mexican, stems and seeds removed
- 1 quart water
- 3/4 pound Roma tomatoes
- 1 cup green unroasted pumpkin seeds
- 1/2 cup finely chopped white onion
- 2 tablespoons olive oil
- 6 cloves garlic, roasted
- 2 canned chipotle chiles in adobo sauce
- 1 teaspoon adobo sauce from
  canned chipotles
- 1/2 cup dry roasted peanuts
- 1 teaspoon ground cinnamon
- 1/2 teaspoon ground allspice
- Pinch ground cloves
- 1 teaspoon sugar
- 1 1/2 teaspoons salt
- 1 tablespoon peanut oil

Preheat the oven to 250 degrees.

Place all the dried chiles on a baking pan and bake in the oven for 10 to 15 minutes or until the chiles smell like they are toasted, being careful not to let them burn. Or toast them on a heavy skillet or comal. Put the dried, toasted chiles in a large pot, cover with 1 quart of water, and simmer for 30 minutes. Set aside and allow to cool.

Roast the tomatoes in a skillet or under a broiler until the skin blackens, then peel them.

Dry roast pumpkin seeds in a pan for about 5 minutes or until they have finished popping. Place in a blender or food processor along with the tomatoes and puree to form a paste.

Saute the onion in the oil until slightly browned. Add the reconstituted dried chiles, about 1/2 cup of chile water if it isn't bitter or use plain water, garlic, chipotles, sauce, peanuts, spices, sugar, and salt to the blender and puree until smooth.

Heat the oil in a heavy pan until it is almost smoking. Fry the sauce for 3 to 5 minutes, stirring continuously.

 Yield: 4 to 5 cups

A Selection of Spectacular Sauces and Salsas

Hot Bean Sauce

Although Asian hot bean sauce is readily available at most supermarkets or specialty shops, it's better to make your own. Use in any recipe requiring bean sauce, hot bean paste, or chile paste. Use as a dip for tempura vegetables, roasted pork slices, deep-fried wontons, or egg rolls.

6 fresh or dried red chiles, such as
   piquins or japones, stems and seeds
   removed, chopped
1 can (15 1/4-ounces) red beans, drained,
   liquid reserved
1/2 cup water, divided
1/2 teaspoon cornstarch
1/4 teaspoon white vinegar
2 cloves garlic, chopped
1 tablespoon vegetable oil
1/8 teaspoon salt

If using dried chiles, place in hot water and soak for 15 minutes or until softened. Drain and chop the chiles.

Place the beans in a blender or food processor and puree until smooth, adding a little of the bean liquid if necessary.

Mix 1 tablespoon of the water with the cornstarch and vinegar and set aside.

Saute the chiles and garlic in the oil until the garlic is browned. Add the beans, salt, and the remainder of the water. Simmer, covered, for 20 minutes.

Uncover, stir in the cornstarch mixture, and simmer for an additional 10 minutes to reduce the liquid.

Store the bean paste in a covered glass jar in the refrigerator where it will keep for 2 to 3 weeks. Stir before using.

 Yield: 2 cups

Chile Quiz, Part 1

Q. Smoking cigarettes in chile fields is often prohibited because: (a) the smoke causes the peppers' stomata to close, inhibiting osmosis; (b) used cigarette ends ("butts") can pollute the soil; (c) an insidious disease known as tobacco mosaic virus may be transmitted; (d) pepper pickers are susceptible to tobacco smoke.

A. (c) Tobacco and chiles are both members of Solanaceae, the Nightshade family. Viruses may be transmitted between various species of this family.

A Selection of Spectacular Sauces and Salsas

Lemongrass Curry Sauce

Richard Sterling, author of Dining with Head-hunters, *collected this recipe during his travels. He wrote, "In Cambodia, as in India, there are as many curries as there are cooks, but all true Khmer curries have five constants: lemongrass, garlic, galangal, and coconut milk; the fifth constant is the cooking technique, dictated by the texture of lemongrass and the consistency of coconut milk. This is my personal, all-purpose, four-cup curry which is based on extensive observation and many trials. To prepare one portion, pour 1/2 cup of this curry sauce into a shallow vessel or a wok. Add 1/2 cup of meat or vegetables, bring to a medium boil, and cook to desired degree. Try it with frog legs as the Cambodians do."*

1 jalapeño chile, stem and seeds removed, chopped

1/3 cup sliced lemongrass*

4 cloves garlic, chopped

3 shallots, chopped

1 teaspoon dried galangal*

1 teaspoon ground turmeric

3 1/2 cups coconut milk

3 lime leaves*

Pinch of salt or shrimp paste*

Place the chile, lemongrass, garlic, shallots, galangal, and turmeric in a blender or food processor and puree until smooth.

Bring the coconut milk to a boil, add the pureed ingredients, lime leaves, and salt, and boil gently, stirring constantly, for 5 minutes. Reduce the heat and simmer, stirring often, for about 30 minutes, or until lime leaves are tender and the sauce is creamy. Remove the leaves.

Yield: 3 cups

Note: If you cannot find coconut milk, you can substitute 4 cups grated dried unsweetened coconut, soaked in a quart of water for an hour and strained.

*Available in Asian markets.

John Thorne in *Cookbook* reported, "Chile peppers are the biggest food craze to hit the American palate since...well, since chocolate. True, garlic and barbecue have had their moments and even their newsletters, but nothing like the spate of cookbooks, press hype, mail-order purveyors, posters, Christmas lights, and other collectibles that has followed in the wake of chilemania."

Very Aromatic Tomato Ginger Jam

Here is a fine jam from Chris Schlesinger of the East Coast Grill in Cambridge, Massachusetts. He noted, "The main features of this jam/condiment are its strength of flavor and the potent aromatic herb combination of lemongrass, basil, cilantro, and mint, which are added at the very end of the preparation so that their flavors are full strength. I have encountered these herbs together in Vietnamese as well as Thai food. I find that this jam has a unique flavor that I'd serve with just about anything grilled."

1 medium onion, thinly sliced

3 tablespoons peanut oil

1 tablespoon minced garlic

2 tablespoons grated ginger

2 large tomatoes, diced

2 tablespoons sugar

3 tablespoons rice wine vinegar

1 tablespoon finely chopped green onions

1 tablespoon finely chopped lemongrass

1 tablespoon finely chopped cilantro

1 tablespoon minced basil

1 tablespoon finely chopped mint

Juice of 1 lime

Juice of 1 lemon

Saute the sliced onion in the oil until browned, about 5 to 7 minutes. Add the garlic and ginger and saute for an additional minute.

Add the tomatoes, reduce the heat, and simmer until as much moisture as possible has been removed but the mixture has not begun to stick to the pan, about 10 minutes. Stir in the sugar and vinegar and cook for 2 minutes.

Remove from the heat and let cool for 15 minutes. Add the green onions, lemongrass, herbs, and the lime and lemon juice; stir until well blended.

The jam will keep up to 10 days, covered, in the refrigerator.

 Yield: about 1 1/2 cups

As reported by Rob McCaleb in *HerbalGram*, in two years there have been more than 650 studies of capsaicin, including 114 clinical studies on humans, mostly concerning the ability of the chemical to inhibit pain.

Chile Verde
(Green Chile Sauce)

Like the red sauce, this all-purpose green chile sauce can be used for enchiladas, green chile and meat, tacos, burritos, or any number of dishes. For a hotter, smoother sauce add some jalapeños and blend. You can eliminate the tomatoes if you are a purist.

1 medium onion, chopped

2 cloves garlic, minced

2 tablespoons vegetable oil, divided

6 to 8 green New Mexican chiles, roasted, peeled, stems and seeds removed, chopped

1 medium tomato, peeled and chopped

1/4 teaspoon ground cumin, optional

2 cups water or chicken broth

2 teaspoons all-purpose flour, divided

Saute the onion and garlic in 1 tablespoon of the oil until soft. Add 1 tablespoon of oil, chiles, tomato, cumin, broth, and 1 tablespoon of flour. Bring to a boil, reduce the heat, and simmer for 30 minutes.

If the sauce is too thin, make a roux with the remaining oil and the flour and saute the mixture for a couple of minutes before adding to the sauce.

 Yield: 2 cups

Indonesian Peanut-Chile Sauce
(Katjang Saos)

Hot and spicy peanut sauce is a standard in this part of the world. This sauce is not only used for sates but is used as a basis for unusual curries and as a dipping sauce as well. It is traditionally prepared by pounding the peanuts into a paste before using. We have simplified the recipe by substituting peanut butter. Serve it with the Sate Kambing (page 19).

4 green onions, chopped, white part only

1 tablespoon peanut oil

4 cloves garlic, minced

1 teaspoon minced ginger

1 cup chicken broth

1 1/2 cups smooth peanut butter

1 tablespoon lime juice, fresh preferred

3 tablespoons crushed red dried New Mexican chiles

1 tablespoon soy sauce

2 teaspoons dark brown sugar

1/4 teaspoon ground cumin

Saute the onions in the oil until soft, add the garlic and ginger, and cook for 3 to 4 minutes. Add the broth, bring to a boil, reduce the heat, and stir in the remaining ingredients. Simmer the sauce, uncovered, for 10 to 15 minutes or until thickened.

Yield: 2 cups

Heat-Infused Salads, Soups, and Stews

Mongolian Noodle Salad

Serve this salad as a first course or as an accompaniment to Asian dinners of all kinds.

Dressing:
- 1/4 cup peanut or vegetable oil
- 2 tablespoons Asian garlic chile-based sauce
- 2 tablespoons cider vinegar
- 1 tablespoon Louisiana-style hot sauce
- 1 tablespoon dark soy sauce
- 1 teaspoon grated ginger
- 1 teaspoon sugar
- 1 teaspoon toasted sesame oil

Salad:
- 2 cups cooked vermicelli or Chinese noodles
- 1/2 cup green onions, chopped including the greens
- 1/2 cup carrots, shredded
- 1/2 cup mung bean sprouts
- 1/4 cup water chestnuts, drained and sliced

Garnish: Chopped peanuts, chopped cilantro

Combine all the ingredients for the dressing, mix well, and allow to sit at room temperature for an hour to blend the flavors.

Place the noodles in a large bowl or platter and top with the vegetables. Pour the sauce over the salad, gently toss, garnish with the nuts and cilantro, and serve.

 Serves: 4 to 6

Southwestern Crab Louis

To this longtime favorite, served with either crab or shrimp, we add two different chiles to heat up the dressing.

Dressing:
- 3 tablespoons prepared red chile sauce
- 4 green New Mexican chiles, roasted, peeled, stems and seeds removed, chopped
- 1/2 cup mayonnaise
- 2 tablespoons lime juice, fresh preferred
- 1 teaspoon prepared horseradish sauce

Salad:
- Mixed salad greens—butterhead, romaine, radicchio, red leaf lettuce
- 1 small onion, thinly sliced and separated into rings
- 3/4 pound cooked crabmeat
- 1 tomato, cut in wedges
- 2 hard-cooked eggs, cut in wedges
- 1 lime, cut in wedges

Garnish: Black olives

Combine all the ingredients for the dressing and let sit for an hour to blend the flavors.

Arrange the salad greens on plates and top with the onion rings. Mound the crab on top and garnish with the olives. Arrange the tomato, egg, and lime wedges around the salad and serve with the dressing on the side.

 Serves: 4

Smoked Salmon and Pasilla Chile Salad

Bob Wiseman who created this recipe told us: "Salmon, in virtually all its forms—steaks, filets, whole, or smoked—is common fare along the Pacific coast, especially in John Steinbeck country, Monterey, California. I like to make this recipe ahead of time, put it in the fridge, and let the subtle flavors mingle for a few hours. If I do say so myself, it's truly an artistic achievement, something Steinbeck would have appreciated."

Dressing:

  1/2 cup olive oil

  2 tablespoons white wine vinegar

  1 tablespoon lime juice, fresh preferred

  2 tablespoons chopped cilantro

  1 teaspoon Louisiana-style hot sauce, such as Tabasco

  1/2 teaspoon ground cumin

  1/2 teaspoon dill seed

  1/2 teaspoon sugar

  1/2 teaspoon salt

  1 clove garlic, minced

  2 dried pasilla chiles, stems and seeds removed

Salad:

  1 small red bell pepper, stem and seeds removed, finely minced

  1/4 cup chopped radishes

  1/4 cup finely diced jicama

  1 cup diced smoked salmon

  1 large head butter lettuce

Garnish: Small white onion sliced in thin rings

Whisk together the oil, vinegar, lime juice, cilantro, hot sauce, cumin, dill, sugar, salt, and garlic in a nonreactive bowl to make a dressing. Cut the pasilla into thin strips, add to the dressing, and refrigerate for 30 minutes

Toss together the bell pepper, radishes, and jicama. Remove the pasilla strips from the dressing and mince. Add the chile to the salad mix. Gently fold in the salmon, being careful not to break it up.

Loosely chop the lettuce in thick shreds and place on chilled salad plates. Top with the salmon mixture, garnish with the onion rings, and serve the dressing on the side.

 Serves: 4

The marketing staff at Kentucky Fried Chicken apparently has underestimated the appeal of fiery foods. Recently the company introduced Hot Wings in an attempt to capitalize on the popularity of "buffalo wings." Fiery food fans flew in to consume the wings in such hordes that the company suspended its national advertising campaign because sales were running fifty percent above projections.

Hearts of Palm Jerk Salad

Hearts of palm are literally the heart of the tender shoots of the palm trees found throughout the Caribbean. The tough outer husks are removed and the insides are boiled until tender. Outside of the Caribbean, you cannot get them fresh. But you can buy them in cans in most supermarkets.

1 teaspoon Dry Jerk Seasoning
2 tablespoons vegetable oil
Juice of 1 lime
1 can hearts of palm, drained, sliced
1 large tomato, sliced
Lettuce

Garnish: Pitted black olives

Whisk the seasoning, oil, and lime juice together.

Arrange the hearts of palm and tomato slices on the lettuce.

Drizzle the dressing over the top, garnish with a couple of olives, and serve.

 Serves: 2

DRY JERK SEASONING

1/2 teaspoon ground habanero chile
1 tablespoon onion powder
1 1/2 teaspoons ground allspice
1 1/2 teaspoons ground thyme
1 teaspoon ground cinnamon
1 teaspoon ground cloves
1/2 teaspoon ground black pepper
1/2 teaspoon garlic powder
1/4 teaspoon ground nutmeg

Combine all the ingredients.

 Yield: 3 tablespoons

In Athens, Ohio, at Ohio University, male students are conducting Saturday Night with the Boys Habanero Eating Contests.

Meanwhile, the Alpha Kappa Alpha Sorority at the University of North Texas was suspended from group activities and five of its members have been convicted of hazing, a misdemeanor, because "pledges were struck with paddles and forced to eat hot peppers."

Gado Gado

This popular Indonesian salad is a meal in itself. Traditionally, the salad is composed of a wide array of raw and parboiled ingredients arranged in layers. It is served with the spicy peanut dressing.

Peanut Dressing:

1 cup peanut butter, smooth or crunchy

1/2 cup water

2 chiltepin chiles, crushed, or substitute piquin or cayenne chiles

2 tablespoons dark soy sauce

1 tablespoon lemon juice

2 teaspoons brown sugar

3/4 teaspoon garlic powder

1/2 to 1 cup coconut milk

Salad:

3 cups mung bean sprouts, brown ends pinched off

1/2 pound green beans, cut into 2-inch pieces

2 large carrots, julienne cut into matchstick size pieces

1 small head cauliflower, separated into small florets

1 large cucumber, skin scored and thinly sliced

2 small potatoes, peeled, boiled, and sliced in 1/4-inch-thick rounds

3 hard-cooked eggs, peeled and quartered

To make the dressing: Combine the peanut butter and water in a saucepan and simmer until combined. Remove from the heat, add all remaining ingredients, and whisk together.

To make the salad: Drop the bean sprouts into boiling water and immediately remove, drain, and rinse under cold water. Boil, steam, or microwave the beans, the carrots, and the cauliflower until only just tender, and rinse under cold water.

To assemble: Arrange potatoes and the vegetables in separate sections on a large platter with egg wedges in the center and the cucumber slices surrounding the platter.

Serve cold with the peanut dressing on the side.

 Serves: 6 to 8

Intrepid chile field botanist Dr. W. Hardy Eshbaugh of Miami University in Ohio reports from Bolivia that his driver stayed awake on long car trips at night by placing crushed ula pica chiles (Capsicum eximium) beneath his cheek and gum...

Kula Greens with Ginger Chile Vinaigrette, Caramelized Macadamia Nuts, and Smoked Marlin

This recipe was given to Melissa Stock by Roger Dikon, executive chef of the Maui Prince Hotel. It indicates a recent trend in Hawaiian food toward hot and spicy.

Dressing:

   3 egg yolks

   1/3 cup minced ginger

   2 tablespoons soy sauce

   2 tablespoons rice wine vinegar

   1 teaspoon dark sesame oil

   1/4 cup macadamia nut honey, or
      substitute regular honey

   3/4 cup macadamia nut oil, or substitute
      peanut oil

   1 teaspoon salt

   1 tablespoon Dijon mustard

   2 fresh piquin chiles, stems and
      seeds removed, minced, or substitute
      serrano chiles

   2 tablespoons water

   Juice of 1 lemon

Caramelized Macadamia Nuts:

   1 tablespoon dark brown sugar

   2 tablespoons water

   3/4 cup diced macadamia nuts, or almonds

Salad:

   1 1/2 cups Kula greens (mixed arugula,
      radicchio, baby lettuce)

   1/2 pound smoked marlin, diced or
      flaked, or substitute other smoked
      white fish or even smoked tuna

   1 cup dried papaya, mango, cherries,
      or raisins

In a blender or food processor, mix the egg yolks, ginger, and soy sauce for 10 seconds. Add the vinegar, sesame oil, honey, nut oil, salt, mustard, and chiles and mix well. Blend or pulse at low speed and slowly add the oil. As the dressing thickens, slowly add the water and lemon juice. Chill before serving.

Heat the sugar in a heavy skillet until it melts. Stir in the water and add the nuts and cook, stirring constantly, until the nuts are sugarcoated and the water has evaporated. Cool to room temperature.

To assemble the salad: Toss the dressing with the greens until well coated. Top with the marlin and dried fruits and garnish with the macadamia nuts.

 Serves: 4

Sea Scallop and Artichoke Heart Salad with Creamy Green Chile Cumin Dressing

This California recipe creatively combines some unusual ingredients to make a very tasty dish. The dressing goes well on lettuce and is also good on cold poached salmon or a chicken breast.

Salad:

1/2 pound scallops

Salad greens such as curly endive, radicchio, arugula, and red leaf lettuce

1 large grapefruit, cut into sections

1 avocado, diced

1 7-ounce jar artichoke hearts

1 small purple onion, thinly sliced

Tomato wedges

Dressing:

3 green New Mexican chiles, stems and seeds removed, chopped

2 cloves garlic, minced

2 tablespoons chopped onion

2 tablespoons lime juice, fresh preferred

1 cup plain yogurt

2 tablespoons mayonnaise

1/4 teaspoon ground cumin

Salt to taste

Bring a large saucepan of water to a boil, add the scallops and when the water returns to a boil, remove from the heat. Drain and rinse under cold water until cool. Cut the scallops into two or three slices. Set aside.

To make the dressing, place the chiles, garlic, onion, and lime juice in a blender or food processor and blend as smooth as possible. Whisk in the remaining dressing ingredients and salt to taste.

Make a bed of greens on four plates. Arrange the grapefruit and avocados on the lettuce, top with the artichokes, scallops, and onions. Garnish with the tomato wedges and serve with the dressing on the side.

 Serves: 4

> "Chiles are a lifestyle. It's an urban cowboy idea of bravado. You have a sense of machismo without running around with a gunrack in the back of your truck. There's got to be a way of proving one's bravado. Chiles are one way of doing that. Chiles will become more popular everywhere. People want—and need—a sense of exoticness." Mark Miller, quoted in the *El Paso Times*, April 26, 1992.

Chicken Salad with Green Chile Mayonnaise

Okay, okay, we admit jazzing up a picnic standard. This spicy chicken salad makes an excellent luncheon entree when served on a bed of shredded lettuce garnished with fresh fruit and whole wheat muffins.

Chicken Salad:
- 4 cups cooked chicken, diced
- 2 stalks celery, chopped fine
- 2 green apples, chopped
- 2 tablespoons walnuts, chopped
- Green Chile Mayonnaise

Combine the ingredients of the salad with the mayonnaise.

 Serves: 4

GREEN CHILE MAYONNAISE

- 3 green New Mexican chiles, roasted, peeled, stems and seeds removed, chopped fine
- 1 cup mayonnaise
- 2 tablespoons minced onion
- 1 teaspoon Dijon-style mustard
- 1/4 teaspoon garlic salt
- Freshly ground black pepper

Combine all the ingredients and let the flavors blend for at least an hour or more.

Yield: 1 cup

An inventor from (where else?) California has invented a process which prevents alcohol from burning off during the cooking process. Hana Chaus, a chemist from Ridgecrest, says the process involves microencapsulating the alcohol contained in beer, but he will not divulge any other details.

"I've made 60-proof chili, 40-proof mayonnaise, and 44-proof bread," said Chaus. "The possibilities are endless."

The legal possibilities are confusing, since the California legislature has never dealt with driving while eating. "Gee, officer, I just had one little bowl..."

Winter Squash and Apple Chowder with Chile-Dusted Croutons

This hearty soup combines several of the fall crops from northern New Mexico, namely, squash, apples, and both red and green chiles. Add a salad, crusty bread, and a nice New Mexican wine and you have a memorable meal.

2 tablespoons butter

1 medium onion, diced

1 1/2 pounds hubbard or butternut squash, peeled, seeds removed, cut into 1-inch cubes

3 tart green apples, such as Jonathans, peeled, cored, and chopped

1/4 cup chopped green New Mexico chiles, stems and seeds removed

1 quart chicken broth

1 teaspoon grated lemon peel

2 tablespoons applejack or Calvados

2 cups cooked, diced chicken

Freshly ground black pepper, to taste

1 to 2 teaspoons cider vinegar (optional)

Saute the onion in the butter until soft. Add the squash and apples and saute for an additional 3 minutes.

Add the chile and stock and bring to a boil. Reduce heat, cover partially, and simmer until the squash and apples are very tender, about 30 to 45 minutes.

Add the lemon peel, chicken, black pepper, applejack, and salt to taste. Simmer for an additional 15 minutes. Add the vinegar if the soup is too sweet.

Top with the croutons and serve.

 Serves: 4 to 6

CHILE-DUSTED CROUTONS

3 slices of white bread, crusts removed, cubed

1 clove garlic, sliced

3 tablespoons butter

2 teaspoons ground red New Mexican chile

1/4 teaspoon ground cumin

Spread the bread cubes on a baking sheet and let them dry out at room temperature for an hour.

Preheat the oven to 300 degrees.

Saute the garlic in the butter for a couple of minutes; remove it and discard. Add the chile and cumin to the butter and quickly toss the bread until all the cubes are coated with the mixture.

Place the cubes back on the baking sheet and bake for 10 minutes or until they are golden brown.

Gulasova Polevka
(Goulash Soup)

"Goulash soup is a favorite throughout Central Europe, from Hungary to the Czech republic to Germany," Sharon Hudgins, who collected this recipe in Czechoslovakia, advised us. The flavor of this soup is even better if you make it one day in advance, then reheat it just before serving. It also freezes well.*

2 medium onions, finely chopped

3 tablespoons vegetable oil

1 pound boneless beef, chuck or arm roast, cut into 1/2-inch cubes

1/4 pound lean bacon, diced

1 green bell pepper, stem and seeds removed, finely diced

1 red bell pepper, stem and seeds removed, finely diced

1 leek, white part only, finely diced

2 potatoes, peeled and finely diced

3 tomatoes, peeled and chopped

6 large cloves garlic, minced

2 tablespoons tomato paste

3 tablespoons sweet (mild) paprika or a mixture of mild and hot paprikas to taste

1 tablespoon caraway seeds

2 teaspoons dried thyme

2 teaspoons dried marjoram

1 teaspoon salt

1 teaspoon freshly ground black pepper

4 to 6 cups water or beef broth

Saute the onions in the oil in a large stock pot until they are browned. Add the beef and bacon and continue to cook until the beef is browned on all sides. Add the bell peppers, leek, potatoes, tomatoes, and garlic and stir well. Stir in the tomato paste, paprika, caraway seeds, thyme, marjoram, salt, and pepper.

Add 4 to 6 cups water, depending on how diluted you want the soup; bring to a boil, reduce the heat and simmer, uncovered, for 1 hour, stirring occasionally. Adjust the seasoning.

Serve hot, accompanied by slices of rye bread.

 Serves: 4 to 6

According to the National Rolaids Heartburn Index, the five worst cities for gas and indigestion, based on consumption of Rolaids, were all in California: Eureka, San Francisco, Chico, Santa Barbara, and Sacramento. The least stressful city in the U.S.: El Paso, Texas. This data explodes the myth of spicy foods causing heartburn.

Sopa de Lima (Lime Soup)

This delicate soup from the Yucatan is popular throughout all of Mexico. Mexican limes, or Key limes, differ from the Persian limes that are common in the United States in that they are smaller, darker green, and more tart than sweet. Although they are preferred, any lime can be substituted.

Vegetable oil for frying

3 corn tortillas, cut in strips

2 chicken breasts

1 small onion, chopped

2 cloves garlic, chopped

6 black peppercorns

1 2-inch stick cinnamon

8 whole allspice berries

1 tablespoon chopped oregano

1 quart chicken broth

1 tomato, peeled and chopped

2 tablespoons lime juice, fresh preferred

1 green New Mexican chile,
   roasted, peeled, stem and seeds
   removed, chopped

4 lime slices

Garnish: Chopped cilantro

Heat the oil to 360 degrees and fry the tortilla strips until crisp. Remove, drain, and keep warm.

Place the chicken, onion, garlic, peppercorns, cinnamon, allspice, oregano, and broth in a pot. Bring to a boil, skimming off any foam that forms, reduce the heat and simmer, covered, for 30 minutes. Allow the chicken to cool in the stock. Remove the chicken and, using two forks, shred the meat. Strain the broth and add enough water to make 1 quart of liquid.

Reheat the broth with the tomato, lime juice, and chile. Add the chicken and simmer until the chicken is hot.

To serve: Place a few of the tortilla strips in the bottom of a soup bowl, add the soup, garnish with a lime slice and chopped cilantro, and serve.

 Serves: 4

Spicy Sweet Potato Soup

Arlene Lutz served us a milder version of this soup on a chile expedition we took to Costa Rica. We added some ground habanero to spice it up, although it is just as good without it. Arlene's secret is to add a little sugar if the potatoes are not sweet enough.

1 quart chicken broth

2 cups diced sweet potato

3 tablespoons orange juice

1/4 teaspoon orange zest

3 tablespoons heavy cream

1/4 teaspoon ground habanero

Pinch of white pepper

Garnish: Chopped parsley

Bring the broth to a boil, add the potatoes, and boil until the potatoes are soft. Place the potatoes and some of the broth in a blender and puree the mixture until smooth.

Combine the puree with the reserved broth and the remaining ingredients. Simmer for 20 minutes.

Garnish with parsley and serve.

 Serves: 4

Sopa de Ajo (Garlic Soup)

Here's a great way for garlic lovers to cram as much of the "stinking rose" as possible into a recipe. The soup will cook the eggs. Richard Sterling gathered this recipe at the Gilroy Garlic Festival.

4 eggs

2 tablespoons olive oil

16 to 20 cloves garlic, coarsely chopped

1 teaspoon crushed red chile

6 cups chicken stock

Juice of 1 lemon

4 slices dry bread, toasted and broken into bite-sized pieces

1/2 cup grated Parmesan cheese

Set the eggs in a bowl of warm water and let them come somewhere above room temperature, but below body temperature.

Heat the oil in a stock pot, add the garlic and chile, and fry for 3 minutes. Add the chicken stock and lemon juice and simmer for 10 minutes.

Gently break an egg into each of four bowls, taking care not to rupture the yolks. Distribute equal amounts of the bread onto the whites of the eggs, leaving the yolks exposed, and sprinkle the cheese evenly over the tops.

Raise the heat under the soup and bring it to a rolling boil. Immediately ladle the boiling soup into the bowls and serve.

 Serves: 4

Bahamian Conch Chowder

Conch Chowder, which is on most menus in the Bahamas, should be tried. Since conch is tough, it is usually tenderized by pounding before being cooked. Conch is available canned. If you are unable to find either fresh or canned conch, try substituting clams.

1 ham bone

2 quarts water

4 conchs, diced

1/4 pound salt pork, cubed

1 tablespoon butter or margarine

1 onion, chopped

1 green bell pepper, stem and
  seeds removed, diced

2 stalks celery, chopped

3 small tomatoes, peeled and diced

3 tablespoons tomato paste

2 large potatoes, diced

2 bay leaves

1 tablespoon chopped fresh thyme

1 carrot, sliced

2 whole cayenne chiles

1 tablespoon dry sherry (optional)

Roux:

2 tablespoons margarine

2 tablespoons flour

Bring the ham and water to a boil, reduce the heat, and simmer for 30 minutes. Add the conch and continue to simmer for 2 hours or until the conch is tender. Remove the ham bone and discard. Set aside the broth with the conch.

Fry the salt pork in butter. Add the onion, green pepper, and celery, and saute until the onion is a light brown, stirring constantly to prevent the mixture from burning. Add the tomatoes and tomato paste; simmer for 1 minute.

Add this sauteed mixture to the pot containing the conch and broth. Add the remaining ingredients, except the roux. Simmer until the vegetables are almost done.

To make the roux, melt the margarine and stir in the flour. Continue to saute and stir to prevent the flour from burning. Cook until the roux is a dark nut-brown color.

Add the roux to the other ingredients and cook for an additional 15 minutes to thicken.

 Serves: 4 to 6

> Best chile pepper quote of the year came from Central American food expert Copeland Marks: "What chiles all have in common is a pungency that is habit-forming and without which food is insipid and without character."

Chile Corn Chowder

This earthy soup, which combines two native Southwestern ingredients, chile and corn, is easy to prepare. It can be made in a crock pot, if you wish.

6 green New Mexican chiles,
    roasted, peeled, stems and seeds
    removed, chopped
3 cups chicken broth
1 potato, peeled and diced
1 onion, chopped
2 cups whole kernel or cream corn
1/2 cup heavy cream
1 cup Monterey Jack or cheddar
    cheese, grated

Combine the chiles, broth, potato, onion, and corn in a pot; bring to a boil, reduce the heat, and simmer until the potatoes are done, about 30 minutes.

Add the cream and cheese and heat until the cheese is melted.

 Serves: 6

Carioca Black Bean Soup

Turtle beans, or black beans, always a favorite in both Central and South America, are gaining in popularity in the United States. All that is needed to complement this hearty soup is some crusty bread and a crisp garden salad.

6 jalapeño chiles, stems and seeds
    removed, chopped
1 large onion, chopped
2 cloves garlic, minced
1 tablespoon vegetable oil
1 1/2 cups black beans, soaked
    overnight, drained
1 large ham hock
1/2 teaspoon ground cumin
6 to 8 cups chicken broth
1 1/2 tablespoons red wine vinegar
2 tomatoes, peeled and diced
2 tablespoons dry sherry
1 tablespoon chopped cilantro

Saute the chiles, onion, and garlic in the oil until soft.

Combine the beans, onion mixture, ham hock, cumin, and broth, bring to a boil, reduce the heat, and simmer until the beans are soft, about 1 1/2 hours. Add the vinegar and tomatoes and simmer for an additional 1/2 hour.

Remove the ham hock, shred the meat, and set aside.

Puree the bean mixture, if desired, until smooth. Return to the saucepan, stir in the sherry, and reheat.

To serve, stir in the shredded ham, top with the cilantro, and serve.

 Serves: 6 to 8

El Patio's Posole with Chile Caribe

According to chef Tom Baca at Albuquerque's El Patio Restaurant, the proper way to prepare posole is to separate the corn and pork from the chile. This allows the diner to adjust the spiciness of the dish and keeps the heat of the chile distinct from the texture and flavor of the hominy corn. Note: For really hot Chile Caribe, add dried piquin chiles, cayennes, or chiles de arbol to the New Mexican chiles.

2 dried red New Mexican chiles, stems
   and seeds removed

8 ounces frozen posole or dried
   posole corn which has been soaked
   in water overnight

1 medium onion, chopped

1 teaspoon garlic powder

3 cups water

1 pound pork loin, cut into 1-inch cubes

Chile Caribe

Garnish: Chopped onions, chopped cilantro

Combine all ingredients, except the pork, in a pot and bring to a boil. Reduce the heat and gently boil for about 3 hours or until the corn is tender, adding more water if necessary. Add the pork and continue cooking for 1/2 hour, or until the pork is tender but not falling apart. The result should resemble a soup more than a stew.

Place the posole in soup bowls and accompany with warmed flour tortillas. The garnishes, Chile Caribe, cilantro, and onions are served in separate bowls. Each guest can then adjust the posole according to individual taste.

 Serves: 4

CHILE CARIBE

6 hot dried red New Mexican chiles,
   stems and seeds removed

1 teaspoon garlic powder

Cover the chiles with water and boil for 15 minutes. Place the chiles, along with the water and garlic, in a blender or food processor and puree until smooth. Transfer to a serving bowl and allow to cool.

 Yield: 1/2 to 3/4 cup

As reported in *The New York Times*, a mother and her daughter were shopping in a store in Great Barrington, Massachusetts, that sells Southwestern apparel and memorabilia.

"What's that, Mommy?" the small child asks, pointing to a ristra of red chiles.

"I don't know, dear," her mother replies. "I think it's part of a dead cow."

Just wait until that little girl sees a chipotle!

Hunter's Stew with Thimble Dumplings

Hunter's stew is a rich dish typical of several regions of the Danube. Wild game may be used to replace the beef. This recipe was collected in the former Yugoslavia by Marge Peterson.

1/2 pound bacon, chopped
2 cups chopped onion
4 dried cayenne-type chiles, stems and
  seeds removed
1 clove garlic, minced
1 cup sliced carrots
2 cups beef stock
2 cups water
1/4 cup red wine
2 pounds chuck beef, cut into
  2-inch cubes
Salt to taste
2 cups potatoes, cut into 1-inch cubes

Fry the bacon until crisp, remove from pan, and drain off all but 1 to 2 tablespoons of the fat. Add the onions and saute until they are soft and translucent. Add the chiles, garlic, and carrots; saute for an additional few minutes.

Return the bacon to the pan, add the broth, water, wine, beef, and salt to taste. Simmer, covered, for 30 minutes. Add the potatoes, cover, and continue to simmer for 20 to 30 minutes or until the potatoes are done and the meat is tender. Adjust the seasonings. Serve with Thimble Dumplings on the side. Italian gnocchi can be substituted.

 Serves: 4

GALUSKA THIMBLE DUMPLINGS

1 egg, beaten
2 cups all-purpose flour
1/8 teaspoon salt
1 quart boiling water

Knead the ingredients together, adding a few drops of water if the dough is too dry. Cut teaspoon-sized pieces off the dough and drop into boiling water. When the dumplings rise to the surface, drain and serve.

North Carolina police trainer John Schneider on capsicum pepper spray: "Whatever your problems were in this world before you were sprayed, you won't think about them for the next thirty or forty minutes."

"Nevada Annie" Harris's 1978 World Championship Chili

This classic recipe won the International Chili Society championship in 1978. The contestants are used to big competitions and cook huge amounts of chile, so exact proportions are not so critical. Home cooks can certainly cut this recipe in half.

3 medium onions, diced

2 green bell peppers, stems and seeds removed, diced

2 large stalks celery, diced

2 small cloves garlic, minced

1 or more jalapeños, stems and seeds removed, minced

2 tablespoons vegetable oil

4 pounds coarsely ground lean chuck

1 7-ounce can diced green chiles

2 3-ounce bottles commercial chili powder

2 14-ounce cans stewed tomatoes

1 15-ounce can tomato sauce

1 6-ounce can tomato paste

2 tablespoons ground cumin

Hot sauce to taste

1 12-ounce can beer

1 12-ounce bottle mineral water, not carbonated

2 to 3 bay leaves

1/4 teaspoon garlic salt

Salt and pepper to taste

In a large stock pot, saute the onions, green peppers, celery, garlic, and jalapeño in the oil until soft. Add the beef and continue to cook until the meat is browned.

Add the remaining ingredients, including 1/2 can beer (drink the remainder, says Annie) and just enough water to cover the top. Bring to a boil, reduce the heat, and simmer for 3 hours, stirring often. Taste and adjust the seasonings.

 Serves: 8 to 12

> Fish tacos are becoming Mexico's latest food fad, served with mayonnaise, shredded cabbage, and—of course—hot salsa.

Dorene Ritchey's 5-R Chili

Dorene Ritchey says the most important ingredient in award-winning chili is luck. However, as a three-time Terlingua champion, we believe there's more than luck involved with her chili. Please note that a great bowl of red is not quickly made. Total cooking time of the recipe is 2 1/2 to 3 hours.

2 pounds beef, chuck or shoulder arm preferred, trimmed and cubed

2 tablespoons vegetable oil

1 1/2 teaspoons hot sauce

8 ounces tomato sauce

2 beef bouillon cubes

2 jalapeños, slit down the side, divided

Spice Mixture:

6 tablespoons ground red New Mexican chile

4 teaspoons ground cumin

1 tablespoon powdered onion

1 teaspoon garlic powder

1/2 teaspoon salt

1/2 teaspoon white pepper

1/2 teaspoon ground cayenne

1/4 teaspoon dried oregano

1 crushed bay leaf

Quickly brown the meat in the oil. Add the hot sauce, tomato sauce, bouillon, 1 jalapeño, and water to cover. Simmer, covered, for 60 minutes, stirring occasionally. Add water as needed and remove the jalapeño when it becomes soft. Squeeze any juice from the chile into the mixture and discard the pulp and seeds. Continue cooking the meat and chiles.

Mix together the ingredients for the spice mixture, then divide it into 3 equal parts. During the last hour of cooking, add 1/3 of the spice mixture and the second jalapeño. Continue cooking, adding water as needed.

During the last half hour of cooking, remove the second chile and squeeze in the juice, discarding the pulp and seeds. Add the second 1/3 of the spice mixture. Continue cooking, adding water as needed.

In the last 15 minutes, add the remaining spice mixture. Taste for seasoning and add more chili powder, cumin, and/or salt if needed during the last 5 minutes.

 Serves: 6

According to one pundit, those hot and spicy retail shops springing up all over the country are "the culinary head-shops of their time."

Zarzuela (Catalan Fish Stew)

Sharon Hudgins collected this recipe in Spain. "Zarzuela (sarsuela in the Catalan language) is a musical term for a type of Spanish operetta—a colorful, witty mixture of song, dance, and theater that was especially popular in the 19th century. This same term has come to be applied to this colorful, flavorful dish that combines several types of seafood with sweet red peppers, tomatoes, onions, and almonds." Serve accompanied by plain boiled rice, crusty peasant bread, a green salad (before or after), and a dry white wine.

2 large onions, coarsely chopped

2 to 3 tablespoons olive oil

4 to 5 large cloves of garlic, minced

2 tablespoons finely chopped *jamón serrano* (Spanish dry-cured raw ham, or substitute prosciutto)

1 tablespoon hot Spanish paprika, or mild paprika mixed with ground cayenne

1 tablespoon mild Spanish paprika

1/2 cup ground almonds

2 large tomatoes, peeled and coarsely chopped

2 red bell peppers, stems and seeds removed, cut lengthwise into strips 1/4 inch wide

1 bay leaf, crumbled

Pinch saffron threads

1/2 cup dry white wine

Juice of 1 lemon

1 1/2 pounds fish fillets (sole, turbot, perch, red snapper, singly or in combination), cut into 2-inch chunks

1 pound shrimp, in the shell

Garnishes: 3 tablespoons chopped parsley, 6 lemon wedges

Saute the onions in oil in a stovetop casserole until they begin to soften. Add the garlic and ham, and continue to saute until the onions are soft. Sprinkle the paprika over the onions, stir well, and let the mixture cook for 2 minutes. Stir in the ground almonds and cook, stirring constantly, for another minute. Add the tomatoes, bell peppers, bay leaf, and saffron. Let the mixture cook 5 minutes, uncovered, over medium heat.

Stir in the wine and lemon juice, add the fish, and bring the mixture to a boil. Reduce the heat and simmer, uncovered, for 10 minutes. Add the shrimp, stir gently to combine, and simmer for another 3 to 4 minutes—not longer or the shrimp will toughen.

Garnish with parsley and lemon wedges and serve immediately.

 Serves: 6

A new capsaicin-based remedy for rheumatism, lumbago, and sciatica is now being sold in Oriental stores. It is Vorwerk "Chilli Brand" Porous Capsicum Plaster…

Mole de Olla Borracho

Mole in Mexican cooking is usually associated with a chocolate/chile sauce but since it means "mixture" in Spanish, it also refers to stews such as this one. This is an unusual dish because some of the ingredients are pureed into a sauce before being added to the stew.

1 1/2 pounds boneless pork, cut
    in 1- to 1 1/2-inch cubes
2 tablespoons vegetable oil
4 or 5 jalapeño chiles, stems and seeds
    removed, chopped
1 medium onion, chopped
1 clove garlic, chopped
1/2 teaspoon ground cinnamon
1/4 teaspoon ground cloves
2 cups chicken broth, divided
1 cup whole kernel corn
2 cups fresh green beans
1 cup beer
2 crookneck or zucchini squash, cubed

Brown the pork in the oil. Set aside.

Place the chiles, onion, garlic, cinnamon, cloves, and 1 cup of the broth in a blender or food processor and puree until smooth.

Add the remaining broth to the browned pork along with the chile mixture, corn, beans, and beer, and simmer for 30 minutes. Add the squash and cook for an additional 30 minutes or until the meat is tender and the vegetables are done. Add more beer if necessary; the stew should be fairly thick.

Serve with warmed flour tortillas.

 Serves: 4

Enchantment Green Chile Stew

This is the beef stew or macaroni and cheese of New Mexico—a basic dish with as many variations as there are cooks. Add a warmed flour tortilla and you have a complete meal.

2 pounds lean pork, cut in
    1 1/2-inch cubes
2 tablespoons vegetable oil
1 large onion, chopped
2 cloves garlic, minced
6 to 8 green New Mexican chiles, roasted,
    peeled, stems removed, chopped
1 large potato, peeled and diced
2 tomatoes, peeled and chopped
3 to 4 cups water
1/4 teaspoon dried oregano,
    Mexican preferred

Brown the pork in the oil, remove, and place in a kettle or stockpot. Add the onion and more oil, if necessary, and saute until it is browned. Add the garlic and cook for an additional couple of minutes. Remove and add to the pork.

Pour a little of the water into the pan, bring to a boil, and deglaze the pan. Pour the pan drippings over the pork. Add all the remaining ingredients and simmer for 1 1/2 to 2 hours or until the meat is very tender and is starting to fall apart.

Serves: 4 to 6

For the Carnivore in Most of Us

South Texas Fajitas

From Texas barbecue expert Red Caldwell comes this border classic, "About 20 years ago, fajitas were 'discovered.' Since then, an awful lot of good meat has been wrecked, and skirt steak—once a 'grinder' item—has risen sharply in price. Because skirt steak doesn't come from a tender quadrant of the carcass, some care is needed to turn it into good food. First, it needs to be marinated to tenderize and flavor it. When slicing fajitas, you'll notice that the grain of the skirt steak all runs the same way. If you'll slice the steak at a 45 degree angle to the grain and hold your knife on a 45 degree angle as well, you'll find that the fajitas are much more tender." Serve the fajitas with flour tortillas, a fresh salsa from Chapter 2, guacamole, and cold beer. You'll notice that Red didn't say anything about chicken fajitas—he says that's a contradiction in terms.

2 to 4 jalapeños, canned or fresh, stems
   removed, sliced

3 tablespoons commercial chili powder

1 teaspoon ground cayenne

1 8-ounce bottle herb and garlic oil-based
   salad dressing

1 12-ounce can of beer,
   preferably Lone Star

1 1/2 teaspoons garlic powder

Juice of 4 Mexican (Key) limes

2 teaspoons cumin seeds

1 large onion, minced

2 tablespoons finely chopped cilantro

1 tablespoon Worcestershire sauce

1 bay leaf

2 to 3 pounds beef skirt steak

Combine all of the marinade ingredients. Place the meat in a nonreactive container, add the marinade, cover, and marinate for 6 to 8 hours, turning the meat occasionally.

Fajitas can be cooked in several ways. If you have the space, smoke the fajitas for about 30 minutes with mesquite, then grill for 4 to 6 minutes per side directly over the fire—mesquite coals being the heat of choice. Baste with the marinade throughout the cooking process. If you need to cook the meat completely on a grill, use a fairly slow fire and cook, covered if possible, for about 10 to 15 minutes per side, basting with the marinade.

 Serves: 4 to 6

Note: This recipe requires advance preparation.

The three biggest markets for Mexican sauces in the U.S. were Los Angeles, San Francisco/Oakland, and Denver, followed closely by Dallas/Ft. Worth, Phoenix/Tucson, and Houston.

Texas Barbecued Brisket

Texas barbecues are legendary, taking hours or even days to cook. Beef brisket is king. First it is covered with a spicy rub, either wet or dry, which coats the meat and helps hold in the juices. The meat is then cooked slowly and basted with a rich sauce during the last hours of cooking. Ideally, the brisket should be smoked over aromatic woods (pecan, apple, etc.) rather than charcoal, but this method will work fine.

1 1/2 pounds mesquite wood
   chips, divided
1 5- to 6-pound beef brisket
1/2 cup cider vinegar
Barbecue Rub:
  1/4 cup ground red New Mexican chile
  2 teaspoons ground cayenne
  2 teaspoons garlic powder
  1 teaspoon ground black pepper
  1/4 teaspoon ground cumin
Basting Sauce:
  1 large onion, chopped
  4 cloves garlic, minced
  1/4 cup vegetable oil
  1/4 cup Worcestershire sauce
  3 tablespoons cider vinegar
  1 12-ounce can beer
  1/2 cup catsup
  2 tablespoons ground red New
    Mexican chile
  4 chiltepins, crushed

Soak the wood chips in water for 2 hours, remove and drain. Prepare a slow charcoal fire in a covered grill and arrange 1/2 of the wood chips on the coals.

Combine the dry ingredients for the rub. Brush the brisket with the vinegar and thoroughly coat the meat with the rub mixture. Place the brisket on the grill, fat side up, over a drip pan. Close the lid and smoke for 2 1/2 to 3 hours, adding more wood chips as needed.

To make the sauce, saute the onion and garlic in a little of the oil until soft. Add the remaining ingredients and simmer for 30 minutes.

Generously brush the brisket with the sauce a couple of times during the last 1 1/2 hours of cooking.

To serve: Heat the remaining sauce, adding additional catsup if necessary. Cut the brisket across the grain and serve with the sauce on the side.

 Serves: 6 to 8

A new California "infusion drink" features vodka, tomatoes, jalapeños, and horseradish, which are allowed to ferment before pouring.

Columbus Pepper Steak

Columbus went looking for peppercorns and found the chile pepper instead. In celebration of his search, this recipe combines both of these for flavor and heat. Less tender cuts of steak will produce truly elegant results since marinating will tenderize the meat. An easy way to crush the peppercorns is to wrap them in a towel and pound them with a hammer.

1 tablespoon whole black peppercorns
1 tablespoon whole white peppercorns
2 rib steaks
2 tablespoons Worcestershire sauce
2 tablespoons soy sauce
2 tablespoons rice vinegar
1 tablespoon habanero-based hot sauce

Roughly crush the peppercorns and then pound them into each side of the steaks. Place in a non-reactive pan.

Combine the remaining ingredients and pour over the steaks, making sure the whole surface (both sides) is covered. Marinate the steaks for 2 hours at room temperature.

Grill or broil the steaks to desired doneness.

 Serves: 2

Jalapeño-Stuffed Steaks

Grilled steaks no longer have to be just pieces of plain meat. They can be stuffed with chiles! Any type of fresh chile or combination of chiles can be substituted for the jalapeños in this recipe. One hour before cooking, slice the steaks and fill with the chile mixture. Allow to come to room temperature before grilling.

Stuffing:
10 jalapeño chiles, stems and seeds removed, chopped
1 medium onion, chopped
4 cloves garlic, minced
1 tablespoon vegetable oil
1/2 cup grated Monterey Jack cheese

2 pounds trimmed filet of beef, cut in 4 thick steaks
Freshly ground black pepper, to taste

Saute the chiles, onion, and garlic in the oil until soft but still a little crisp. Remove, cool, and mix in the cheese. Refrigerate this stuffing a day before you use it.

Slice into the steaks from the edge, creating a pocket for the stuffing. Stuff with the jalapeño mixture and fasten the opening with a toothpick, if necessary. Season the outside of each steak with the black pepper.

Grill over hot charcoal to desired doneness.

 Serves: 4

Note: This recipe requires advance preparation.

Carne Asada Tacos with Molcajete Sauce

You can use skirt steaks (fajita meat) or the more traditional tenderloin to make carne asada.

1 pound beef skirt steak or tenderloin
Juice of 1 lime, Mexican (Key)
   lime preferred
2 to 3 tablespoons vegetable oil
Salt to taste
8 flour tortillas
Garnishes: Lettuce, diced tomatoes,
   guacamole
Molcajete Sauce

Place the meat in a nonreactive dish, squeeze the lime juice over the top, and marinate for 3 hours in the refrigerator.

Heat the oil in a skillet until quite hot and fry the skirt steak quickly. Allow the steak to rest for 15 minutes in a warm oven. If you use tenderloin instead of skirt steak, before you fry it, slice the meat with the grain into several small steaks.

Before serving, slice the meat with the grain into strips 1/4-inch thick and season with salt. Mix the sliced meat with the sauce.

To serve: Heat the tortillas by placing them on a hot, dry skillet, one at a time, turning them frequently until hot. Wrap the meat in the tortillas and serve with the garnishes.

Serves: 4

Note: This recipe requires advance preparation.

Molcajete Sauce

A molcajete is a mexican mortar.

2 large tomatoes
2 jalapeños, stems and seeds removed,
   minced, or 6 dried piquin chiles, stems
   removed, crushed
1 onion, diced
2 cloves garlic, minced
Juice of 2 limes
Salt to taste

Roast the tomatoes in a dry skillet or a comal until the skin is a little charred. Do not peel.

Place all the sauce ingredients in a molacajete or blender and process into a sauce. Season to taste with the salt and serve.

 Yield: 1 to 1 1/2 cups

Cheery medical note from the scientific journal Toxicon: drinking about a quart and a half of Louisiana hot sauce will cause death by respiratory failure if your body weight is 140 pounds or less.

Grilled Flank Steak with Pecans, Black Beans, and Cilantro

Flank steak is another cut of beef that needs tenderizing by marinating. This recipe, a favorite at the Routh Street Cafe in Dallas, was published in Chile Pepper when chef Stephan Pyles was featured in "Chile Chefs from Coast to Coast."

Marinade:

1 3/4 cups dry red wine, divided

3/4 cup corn oil

2 tablespoons soy sauce

3 tablespoons chopped fresh
   cilantro, divided

2 jalapeño chiles, stems
   removed, chopped

5 cloves garlic, 3 chopped, 2 left whole

1 tablespoon coarsely ground
   black pepper

1 1/2 to 2 pounds flank steak

1/3 cup pecan halves

4 serrano chiles, stems removed, chopped

1/4 cup unsalted butter or
   margarine, divided

1 tablespoon minced chives

1/3 cup chicken broth

1/3 cup red wine vinegar

1 large shallot, chopped

1 teaspoon lime juice, fresh preferred

1/4 cup canned or cooked black beans,
   drained and rinsed

Salt and pepper to taste

Warm flour tortillas

Combine 1 1/2 cups wine, oil, soy sauce, 2 tablespoons cilantro, jalapeños, chopped garlic, and the coarse black pepper and mix well. Place the steak in a nonreactive pan, cover with the marinade, and marinate in the refrigerator for at least 2 hours or overnight.

Preheat the oven to 350 degrees.

Toast the pecans in the oven until lightly browned, about 5 minutes. Remove and set aside.

Rub the remaining 2 whole garlic cloves with a little butter and roast in the oven until soft and light brown, about 20 minutes.

Crush the pecans, roasted garlic, and serrano chiles together in a mortar or bowl. Blend in 2 tablespoons of the butter and the chives.

Preheat a grill or the broiler.

Combine the stock, remaining wine, vinegar, shallot, lime juice, and 1 tablespoon of the cilantro. Bring to a boil, stirring constantly, until it is reduced to 2 tablespoons. Reduce the heat and whisk in the remaining butter, a little at a time. Stir in the black beans and season the sauce with salt and pepper to taste. Add the pecan mixture and keep the sauce warm.

Remove the steak from the marinade. Lightly brush it with a little of the marinade and season with salt and pepper. Grill the steak over a moderately hot fire or broil until medium rare, 5 to 7 minutes.

To serve: Thinly slice the steak crosswise on the diagonal and arrange on warmed plates. Spoon the sauce over each serving and accompany with warm flour tortillas.

 Serves: 4 to 6

Red Centre Meatballs

This interesting hot and spicy Australian recipe was collected by Sally Hammond, who commented: "The arid inland desert area of Australia is often referred to as the 'red centre.' Hence the name of this recipe. These meatballs, which can be made with lean ground beef, have a hot, red centre too." Serve with hot steamed rice or cooked noodles or with a salad from Chapter 3.

2 sun-dried tomatoes, rehydrated
   and minced
2 tablespoons fine bread crumbs
1 clove garlic, crushed
1 tablespoon crushed dried red chiles
   such as piquins, chiltepins, or japones
1 tablespoon chopped cilantro
1 teaspoon grated ginger
Salt
1 pound lean ground beef or kangaroo meat
Vegetable oil for frying

Combine the tomatoes, bread crumbs, garlic, chiles, cilantro, ginger, and a little salt and mix well. Pinch off egg-size pieces of meat or smaller and flatten them in the palm of your hand. Place a small amount of the chile mixture in the center and roll up carefully to close. Continue until all the meat and filling are used.

Place the oil in a frying pan to a depth of an inch, heat and fry the meatballs, turning constantly until browned and cooked through. Remove and drain.

 Serves: 4

Classic Carne Adovada

This traditional New Mexican dish demonstrates our love of chile. Simple, easy, and tasty, it is basically pork marinated in a hot chile sauce. It can be eaten plain as an entree or wrapped in a flour tortilla as a burrito.

18 to 24 dried red New Mexican chiles,
   stems removed
3 cups water or chicken broth
4 cloves garlic
2 teaspoons dried oregano
3 pounds lean pork, cut in strips

Cover the chiles with water or broth and simmer for 10 minutes or until softened. Place the drained chiles, garlic, and oregano in a blender or food processor along with just enough of the chile water and puree to make a sauce. The sauce should be thick.

Marinate the pork in the sauce overnight.

Preheat the oven to 300 degrees.

Bake the pork in the marinade, covered, for a couple of hours or until the meat is very tender and starts to fall apart. Uncover during the last 1/2 hour of cooking to slowly bake off the excess liquid.

 Serves: 4 to 6

Sichuan Tangerine Beef

This recipe incorporates four distinctive Sichuan ingredients—chile paste, chile peppers, Sichuan peppercorns, and tangerines—as well as a distinctive method of beef preparation. Crispy fried beef is dry and chewy and the flavor more concentrated, requiring a highly seasoned multiple-flavored sauce such as this. Pork and chicken are also delicious in this recipe. If you cannot find tangerines, substitute oranges.

5 piquin or other small hot peppers

2 teaspoons crushed Sichuan peppercorns

2 teaspoons minced ginger

2 cloves garlic, minced

1/2 cup tangerine or orange juice

2 tablespoons dark soy sauce

1 tablespoon hoisin sauce

1 teaspoon sugar

3/4 teaspoon Asian garlic chile paste

2 eggs

3 tablespoons cornstarch

1 1/2 pounds beef, sirloin or top round, cut in thin strips

1/2 cup vegetable oil, peanut preferred

2 tablespoons tangerine or orange peel, cut in strips

1 teaspoon rice wine vinegar

Combine the chile, peppercorns, ginger, and garlic in a bowl. In another bowl combine the juice, soy sauce, hoisin sauce, sugar, and chile paste, and mix well. Set aside.

Mix together the eggs and cornstarch and toss the beef strips in the mixture until well coated. Heat the oil in a wok or heavy skillet and stir-fry the beef for 2 minutes or until crispy. Remove and drain. Pour out all but 1 tablespoon of the oil.

Reheat the oil and stir-fry the chile pepper mixture for 30 seconds. Add the tangerine peel and the juice mixture and stir-fry for an additional 15 seconds.

Return the beef to the wok, add the vinegar, and continue to cook until thoroughly heated.

Serve over a bed of white rice.

Serves: 4 to 6

Medical researchers at the National Institute of Allergy and Infectious Diseases have developed a nasal spray which stops gustatory rhinitis, that dreaded draining of the nasal passages caused by eating hot chiles. The condition, sometimes called the "salsa sniffles," is caused by overstimulated nerves and is unlike the runniness associated with head colds or allergies, which is triggered by a histamine reaction.

Stir-Fry Beef with Crispy Bean-Thread Noodles

This is a cross between two classic Chinese dishes: Ants Climbing a Tree and Mongolian Beef. We like using the bean-thread noodles because they sit in the oil for a couple of seconds and then suddenly expand to fill the pan with puffed-up noodles.

2/3 pound flank steak

1 tablespoon dark soy sauce

2 teaspoons rice wine or dry sherry

2 teaspoons sugar

1/2 teaspoon crushed
   Sichuan peppercorns

2 teaspoons toasted sesame oil

1 tablespoon minced ginger

3 large cloves garlic, minced

6 dried piquin or small cayenne chiles

1 tablespoon hoisin sauce

1/4 cup chicken stock or canned broth

1 1/2 cups peanut oil

1 1/2 ounces dried bean-thread noodles

6 green onions, sliced, including
   the green tops

Place the beef in the freezer for 15 to 20 minutes. Remove and slice it lengthwise across the grain into 1/8-inch-thick strips.

Mix the soy sauce, wine, sugar, peppercorns, and sesame oil to form a marinade. Toss the beef in the marinade and marinate for an hour.

Combine the ginger, garlic, and chiles in one bowl, with the hoisin sauce and broth in another.

Heat the peanut oil until it is very hot and fry the noodles in small batches; heat until they puff, about 3 to 5 seconds. Remove the noodles and drain.

Pour off all but 1 to 2 tablespoons of the oil and reheat. Add the ginger mixture and stir-fry for 30 seconds. Add the meat and stir-fry until browned, about 2 minutes. Push the meat to the side of the pan.

Stir in the hoisin sauce mixture and bring to a boil. Simmer for a minute to blend. Add the onions and beef and heat through.

Pour the meat over a bed of noodles, garnish with some onions, and serve.

 Serves: 4

A 1994 Red Savina Habanero from GNS Spices has tested an astonishing 577,000 Scoville Units and is believed to be the hottest pepper ever tested.

The Journal of the American Medical Association reported that a team of doctors at the Baylor College of Medicine in Houston conducted a unique experiment utilizing videoendoscopy, the high-tech procedure of inserting a fiber-optic tube and a miniature video camera into the stomach to inspect it visually.

The object of the experiment was to test the generally-held theory that capsaicin, the active heat chemical in chile peppers, damages the lining of the stomach. The research team, led by Dr. David Graham, subjected 12 volunteers (none were chile lovers) to a series of test meals—bland, plain aspirin, "Mexican," and pizza. After each meal, the endoscope was inserted to determine if "gastric erosions" of the lining had occurred. By far, the most damaging meal was the bland one combined with aspirin.

Not believing their results, the research team then sprayed Tabasco sauce directly on the stomach lining. There was mucosal damage this time, but it was linked to the vinegar in the sauce. To further test capsaicin alone, the good doctors then injected 30 grams of freshly ground jalapeños directly into the stomach. There was no visible mucosal damage.

Dr. Graham concluded in his study: "We found that ingestion of highly spiced meals by normal individuals did not cause endoscopically demonstrable gastric or duodenal mucosal damage." However, in an interview published in the *Los Angeles Times,* Dr. Graham admitted that chiles increase gastric acid secretion, but "they add to the flavor and enjoyment of eating and do not appear to cause stomach lining damage."

Dixie Bourbon-Glazed Ribs

In the South, the barbecue meat of choice is pork and hickory is the most commonly used wood, but opinions are split on the correct sauce. The cooks in Georgia prefer a sweet tomato-based sauce, while those in Tennessee swear by a vinegar-based sauce. The following is a compromise, with the tang of vinegar and a hint of sweetness—and a little heat.

3 to 4 cups hickory chips

Sauce:

  1 cup minced onion

  1/3 cup vegetable oil, divided

  2/3 cup bourbon

  1/2 cup cider vinegar

  1/2 cup orange juice

  2 tablespoons Worcestershire sauce

  1 tablespoon dry mustard

  1 tablespoon grated orange peel

  1 tablespoon crushed red New Mexican chile

  1/2 teaspoon freshly ground black pepper

4 pounds pork ribs

Soak the wood chips for 2 hours, drain. Prepare a slow fire in a covered grill. Arrange the wood chips on the coals.

To make the sauce, saute the onion in a tablespoon of the oil. Combine the remaining sauce ingredients, bring to a boil, reduce the heat, and simmer for 5 to 10 minutes. Allow the sauce to sit for an hour to blend the flavors.

Place the ribs on the grill, fat side up, over a drip pan. Close the lid and grill for 1 1/2 to 2 hours, adding more wood chips if necessary. Brush the ribs with the sauce every 30 minutes during the last half of the cooking.

 Serves: 4

Angry Pork Tenderloin

Dennis Hayes collected this recipe from chef Joey Altman of Miss Pearl's Jam House, which is one of our favorite places to dine in San Francisco. Serve the pork with black beans, rice, a salsa (see Chapter 2), and tortillas.

4 dried or canned chipotle chiles

12 cloves of garlic (yes, 12!)

3 shallots

1 tablespoon ground allspice

5 whole cloves

1/2 cup malt vinegar

1/2 cup orange juice

1/4 cup lime juice

1/4 cup brown sugar

1 teaspoon freshly ground black pepper

1 1/2 cups olive oil

2 pork tenderloins, trimmed of excess fat

If using dried chipotles, cover with hot water for 15 minutes to soften. Remove the stems.

Place all ingredients except the oil and tenderloins in a blender or food processor and puree while slowly drizzling in the oil. Marinate the meat in this marinade for at least an hour.

Remove the pork from the marinade and grill over medium-high heat or bake in a 400-degree oven for about 8 minutes, turning every 2 minutes.

Slice the tenderloins into 1/2-inch pieces and serve.

 Serves: 4

Grilled Marinated Pork Tenderloin with Roasted Corn and Poblano Chile Relish

This recipe, from the "Hot Spots" department of the magazine, features a great new Southwest creation by Chef de Cuisine David Jones of La Casa Sena in Santa Fe. This historic restaurant is housed in the José Sena classic adobe structure that was built in the late 1860s.

The Pork Tenderloin:

  2 jalapeño chiles, stems and seeds
     removed, chopped
  1/2 cup sherry vinegar
  1 cup olive oil
  1 teaspoon chopped garlic
  1 teaspoon chopped shallots
  1 teaspoon ground cumin
  1 teaspoon salt
  4 pork tenderloins, trimmed of excess fat

Combine the jalapeños, vinegar, oil, garlic, shallots, cumin, and salt in a nonreactive bowl. Add the pork and marinate in the refrigerator for 3 hours.

Remove the pork from the marinade and grill or broil until it is just done, about 7 to 8 minutes per side.

Slice the pork into medallions and fan out on individual serving plates. Carefully spoon out the Roasted Corn and Poblano Chile Relish on the medallions so that they are half covered.

 Serves: 4

ROASTED CORN AND POBLANO CHILE RELISH

  2 poblano chiles
  1 red bell pepper
  2 ears corn
  1 teaspoon vegetable oil
  3 tablespoons finely chopped shallots
  3 tablespoons minced garlic
  1 bunch fresh cilantro, chopped
  1/2 cup olive oil
  1/3 cup sherry vinegar
  Salt and pepper to taste

Lightly brush the poblanos, bell pepper, and corn with the oil and roast them over a gas flame until the skin is blackened. Peel the chiles, remove the stems and seeds, and dice the chiles. Cut the kernals off the corn cob.

Combine all the ingredients, including the corn kernals for the relish, mix well, and allow to sit for at least 2 hours to blend the flavors.

Sweet and Hot Lamb with Plum Glaze

Glazes or sauces that have a high percentage of sugar should be used only during the last third of the grilling time and only with a medium-warm fire or the sugar will burn. We also use this sauce with beef.

1 16-ounce can purple plums, pitted and
    drained, reserving the syrup
2 tablespoons honey
2 tablespoons white vinegar
1 tablespoon soy sauce
1 tablespoon crushed red pepper
2 cloves garlic
1 teaspoon minced ginger
1 pound lamb, cut in
    1 1/2- to 2-inch cubes
Skewers

Puree the plums in a blender or food processor. Place the plums and the remaining ingredients, except the lamb, in a saucepan and bring to a boil. Reduce the heat and simmer for 15 minutes, adding 3/4 to 1 cup of the reserved syrup to keep the sauce from becoming too thick.

Thread the lamb on skewers and grill over charcoal, basting with the sauce toward the end of the grilling.

Serve the lamb with a bowl of the remaining sauce for dipping.

 Serves: 4

Pungent Pork Vindaloo

Vindaloo describes a style of cooking whereby the meat is marinated in a vinegar-based sauce and cooked in that marinade. This recipe can also be used for beef or lamb. Add ground cayenne to the recipe if more heat is desired.

1 tablespoon ground New Mexican chile
1/2 cup cider vinegar
3 tablespoons vegetable oil, divided
2 teaspoons ground cumin
1 teaspoon ground ginger
1/4 teaspoon ground cloves
1/4 teaspoon ground cinnamon
1/4 teaspoon ground turmeric

1 1/2 pounds cubed pork
1 medium onion, chopped
2 cups chicken broth
Garnish: Chopped cilantro

Combine the chile, vinegar, 2 tablespoons of oil, cumin, ginger, cloves, cinnamon, and turmeric to make the marinade. Toss the pork in the mixture and marinate overnight. Remove the pork and reserve the marinade.

Brown the pork in the remaining oil. Add the onion and continue to saute until the onion is browned.

Add the marinade and broth, bring to a boil, reduce the heat, and simmer until the meat is very tender and the liquid is absorbed.

Serve on white rice garnished with the cilantro.

 Serves: 4

Cochinita Pibil
(Pork Cooked in the Pibil Method)

This pre-Columbian dish is probably the best known food of the Maya. It is also one of the most popular entrees in Yucatan on virtually every menu. The Maya used wild boar for this dish until the Spanish began to domesticate pigs. This dish is traditionally served with warmed corn tortillas, black beans, and cebollas encuridas (marinated onions) and a habanero salsa (see Chapter 2).

10 whole black peppercorns

1/4 teaspoon cumin seeds

5 cloves garlic

3 tablespoons Recado Rojo (see page 69)
    or substitute achiote paste

1 teaspoon dried oregano, Mexican
    preferred

2 bay leaves

1/3 cup bitter orange juice (see page 11)
    or substitute 1/3 cup lime juice,
    fresh preferred

Banana leaves* or aluminum foil

2 pounds lean pork, cut in
    1 1/2- or 2-inch cubes

3 xcatic chiles, stems and seeds removed,
    cut in strips, or substitute banana,
    yellow wax, or guero chiles

1 large purple onion, sliced

Place the peppercorns and cumin seeds in a spice or coffee grinder and process to a fine powder. Add the garlic and continue to grind. Combine the spice mixture, recado, oregano, bay leaves, and orange juice. Pour the marinade over the pork and marinate for 3 hours or overnight.

Preheat the oven to 325 degrees.

Cut the banana leaves or aluminum foil in pieces to fit a roasting pan. Soften the leaves by passing them over a gas flame or holding over an electric burner for several seconds until the leaves begin to turn light green. Remove the center ribs from the leaves and use for tying. Lay a couple of strings (long enough to tie around the pork) along the bottom of the pan. Line the pan with the banana leaves or foil.

Place the pork, including the marinade, on the leaves and top with the chiles and onion. Fold the banana leaves over and tie with the banana strings or real string. Cover the pan and bake for 1 1/2 hours.

 Serves: 4 to 6

*Available in Latin and Asian markets, frozen.

Note: This recipe requires advance preparation.

RECADO ROJO

4 tablespoons ground annatto seeds

1 tablespoon dried oregano,
   Mexican preferred

10 whole black peppercorns

1/2 teaspoon salt

1 stick cinnamon (1-inch)

4 whole cloves

2 whole allspice berries

1/2 teaspoon cumin seeds

3 cloves garlic, chopped

3 tablespoons white vinegar

Place the annatto, oregano, peppercorns, salt, cinnamon, cloves, allspice, and cumin in a spice or coffee grinder and process to a fine powder. Add the remaining ingredients and grind to a thick paste, adding a little water if the mixture is too thick.

Allow to sit for an hour or overnight to blend the flavors.

Yield: 1/2 cup

Sylva Carlson, in a letter to *Cook's* magazine, reports that she smears cream cheese on her hands to ease the sting of jalapeños.

Fiery Hot Chorizo

There are hundreds of variations of chorizo—fresh, dried, and smoked versions—throughout Spain, Portugal, and Mexico. Some recipes include wine, almonds, tomatillos, cinnamon, or fresh chiles. Paprika is what gives chorizo its familiar orange color.

1 tablespoon crushed red piquin chile

1 pound ground pork butt

1 pound ground beef chuck

1/4 teaspoon liquid smoke

3 tablespoons red wine vinegar

2 cloves garlic, crushed

1 teaspoon salt

3/4 teaspoon coarsely ground
   black pepper

2 teaspoons brown sugar

1 1/2 teaspoons dried oregano

1 teaspoon ground cumin

2 teaspoons ground paprika

Combine all ingredients and, using your hands, mix well. Refrigerate for at least 30 minutes to blend the flavors. Form into patties.

If making sausage links, add 1/4 cup texturized vegetable protein and 1/2 cup water or beef stock. Fill the casings with the mixture and twist into 8-inch links.

To cook the links, boil for 10 seconds in a small amount of water, drain off the remaining water, then fry until brown in a skillet, adding a little oil if necessary.

Yield: 2 pounds or about 12 to 14 sausages.

For the Carnivore in Most of Us

Rodrigo's Biscuits and Gravy

From Bob Wiseman comes this very different recipe for biscuits and gravy. He gave the history of the recipe: "Back in the fifties I was a lean sprout working as a cook's helper in a lumber camp a short shinny into the Teton Mountains out of Jackson Hole, Wyoming. Nearly every morning, Rodrigo, the camp cook, would brew up a batch of biscuits and gravy. Rodrigo hailed from Silver City, New Mexico, and the Sonoran influence was scattered throughout his recipes. Working with Rodrigo set my mind straight on the value of chiles in cooking; either you liked them or you didn't eat. Consequently, I acquired my taste for chiles on the 'must system' (one must eat). Rodrigo's original biscuits and gravy recipe went with him when they closed the lumber mill. Fortunately, I remembered 'the basics' as I've detailed here."

- 1/2 pound sausage, crumbled
- 3 green onions, chopped, including some of the green tops
- 1/2 cup diced green New Mexican chile, either fresh or canned
- 1 clove garlic, minced
- 1 teaspoon ground sage
- 1/4 teaspoon ground cayenne
- 1/2 teaspoon commercial chili powder
- 3/4 cup all-purpose flour
- 1 cup beef broth
- 2 cups milk
- Salt
- Biscuits or thick slices of toasted sourdough bread
- Garnish: Chopped cilantro, chopped pimento

Saute the sausage in a heavy skillet until brown, remove, and drain on paper towels. Add the green onions, green chile, and garlic to the drippings and cook for a minute or two. Skim off excess fat.

Reduce the heat and return sausage to the skillet. Stir in the sage, cayenne, and chili powder. Sprinkle the flour evenly over the mixture, stir to coat, and cook for a minute.

Add broth, milk, and salt. Stir constantly until the gravy starts to bubble. Reduce the heat and simmer a couple of minutes until the gravy thickens.

Split the biscuits in half, pour the gravy over them, and garnish with the cilantro and pimentos.

 Serves: 4 dudes or 2 Arizona wranglers

> Best recent chile quote from John Yemma, writing in the *Boston Globe:* "Without beets and rhubarb, the food chain would still have ample diversity. Life would go on without turnips. But take away Jalapeños and green and red chiles and serrano and habanero peppers and this would be a cold, mean world..."

Tamarind Pork Chops

In the dictionary under the word tangy *is a picture of this dish. Well, not really, but if there were, you'd be well aware of the definition after eating this dish! Remember to remove the balls on the top of whole cloves, since they are bitter.*

- 2 tablespoons peanut oil
- 4 boneless pork chops, trimmed of fat
- 1 teaspoon whole black peppercorns
- 12 whole cloves
- 3 3-inch cinnamon sticks, crushed
- 8 whole cardamom pods, crushed
- 1 teaspoon chopped garlic
- 1 teaspoon Sambal Oelek (Indonesian chile paste)
- 1 cup water
- 1 teaspoon salt
- 1 tablespoon tamarind paste dissolved in 2 tablespoons boiling water
- 1 teaspoon sugar

Heat the oil in a large skillet and brown the pork chops on both sides. Remove and set aside.

Lower the heat and add the peppercorns, cloves, cinnamon, cardamom, garlic, and Sambal Oelek. Saute the spices for 1 minute, stirring constantly.

Return the pork chops to the skillet, add 1 cup of water and the salt, and stir well. Bring to a boil, reduce the heat, cover, and simmer for 1/2 hour, turning the chops over a couple of times as they cook. Add the tamarind paste/water mixture and sugar. Mix well. Cover and cook about 15 minutes longer or until the chops are fully cooked.

 Serves: 4

Lamb and Cayenne Kefta

Keftas are meatballs prepared with ground lamb or beef and a number of different herbs and spices. They appear in a variety of dishes such as stews and also as brochettes served hot off the charcoal grill in flat Arab or pita bread. The seasonings range from chile peppers to cinnamon and usually include another Moroccan favorite, fresh mint. To serve, remove from the skewers, place in a split piece of pita bread, and serve as a sandwich.

- 1 pound ground lamb
- 1 onion, finely chopped
- 2 tablespoons chopped fresh mint
- 2 teaspoons ground cayenne
- 1 teaspoon ground cloves
- 1 teaspoon ground allspice
- 1 teaspoon ground ginger
- 1 teaspoon ground cardamom
- 1/2 teaspoon ground nutmeg
- 1/2 teaspoon ground cinnamon
- 1/2 teaspoon ground cumin
- **Freshly ground black pepper**
- **Skewers**

Combine all the ingredients and allow to sit at room temperature for 1 hour to blend the flavors.

Shape the meat into 1-inch meatballs and thread on skewers. Either flatten them slightly to make sausage shapes or leave them as balls. Grill the keftas over charcoal or under the broiler to desired doneness.

 Serves: 4

Curried Cashew Lamb with Coriander

Although this recipe calls for lamb, beef or pork can be substituted. The blend of the spices is called a masala and since water is added in this recipe during the blending, it is called a wet masala.

1 teaspoon ground cinnamon

8 small dried chiles such as piquins, stems removed

6 whole cloves

2 tablespoons coriander seeds

1 tablespoon cumin seeds

1 tablespoon chopped ginger

2 teaspoons ground turmeric

1 cup water

1 large onion, chopped

6 cloves garlic, chopped

3 tablespoons vegetable oil

2 pounds boneless lamb, cut in 1 1/2- to 2-inch cubes

2 small tomatoes, peeled, seeds removed, chopped

1 tablespoons chopped cilantro,

Garnish: 1 tablespoons chopped cilantro, 1/2 cup toasted cashews

Combine the cinnamon, chiles, cloves, coriander, cumin, ginger, and turmeric in a spice grinder or blender and process to a powder. Add the water and blend to form a masala or paste.

Saute the onion and garlic in the oil until soft. Add the lamb and brown the meat. Add the spice mixture and tomatoes, bring to a boil, reduce the heat, cover, and simmer for 30 minutes.

Add 1 tablespoon cilantro and water if necessary; continue to simmer for an additional 30 minutes or until the lamb is very tender.

Garnish with the remaining cilantro and cashews, and serve over rice.

Serves: 4 to 6

> "The chiltepin, used ceremonially and privately, is thought to drive away approaching sickness. The man who does not eat chile is immediately suspected of being a sorcerer."
> —a Tarahumara Indian quoted by Wendell Bennett in his book, *The Tarahumara: An Indian Tribe of Northern Mexico.*

Hill Country Venison Steaks with Chile Wine Sauce

Game is very popular in Texas despite the fact that there is very little public land open for hunting in the state. To fill this void, hunters pay ranchers and other private landholders for the right to hunt on their property. If venison is not available, beef or lamb can be substituted in this recipe.

8 crushed chiltepins or other
  small hot chile
1/2 cup dry red or port wine
1/4 cup white vinegar
1/4 cup vegetable oil
2 cloves garlic, minced
1 tablespoon crushed fresh rosemary
Freshly ground black pepper
2 venison steaks, 1 1/2 to 2 inches thick

Combine all the ingredients, except the venison, and marinate the meat in this marinade for 24 hours. Remove the meat and reserve the marinade.

Prepare a charcoal fire. Rub the steaks with a little oil and quickly sear them to hold in the juices. Grill the steaks, basting frequently with the marinade until done.

Serves: 4

Note: This recipe requires advance preparation.

Piñon Grilled Lamb Chops

This marinade is a wonderful blend of the flavors of New Mexico: piñons, chiles, and lamb. Piñons are pine nuts, readily available now since they are imported from China.

1 tablespoon ground New Mexican chile
1/4 cup roasted piñon nuts
3 cloves garlic
1/2 cup tomato paste
1/4 cup olive oil
3 tablespoons lemon juice or vinegar
2 pounds thick-cut lamb chops

Place all the ingredients, except the lamb, in a blender or food processor and puree to make a sauce. Paint the chops with this mixture and let stand at room temperature for an hour.

Grill the chops over a charcoal and piñon wood fire until done, basting with the remaining marinade.

Serves: 4

Life in New Mexico Department: Dave was savoring his weekly ritual lunch with Wayne Scheiner at El Norteño, Albuquerque's great northern Mexican restaurant, when a woman staggered by and knocked over our bucket of bottles of Negra Modelo. "Sorry," she said, "I've got chile in my eye."

Classic Three-Meat Jambalaya

Correspondent Ed Ward collected this recipe in the bayou country. He observed: "Don't ask me why, but it is essential to observe the sauteing and boiling times here assidulously." The three meats are chicken and two Cajun sausages, which are available at specialty stores and by mail order.

3 tablespoons vegetable oil
1 pound lean pork or chicken, diced
2 large onions, finely chopped
1/4 pound tasso, diced (spicy Cajun smoked ham)
5 to 8 cloves garlic, minced
2 bay leaves
1 tablespoon chopped fresh parsley
1 teaspoon dried thyme
1/2 teaspoon ground cloves
1 pound smoked garlic sausage, diced
3 cups beef or chicken broth
1 1/2 cups rice
6 to 8 small hot red chiles, such as piquins, crushed
1 teaspoon ground cayenne
1 teaspoon Ortego, Tabasco, or other Louisiana-type hot sauce
Salt and freshly ground black pepper

Heat the oil in a large pot, add the pork and onions, and saute until the onions are soft and the meat is browned. Add the tasso, garlic, bay leaves, parsley, thyme, and cloves and saute for 5 minutes. Stir in the sausage and continue to cook for an additional 5 minutes.

Add the broth, bring to a boil, and gently boil for 10 minutes. Add the remaining ingredients, bring back to a boil, lower the heat, and simmer for 15 to 20 minutes, uncovered, stirring occasionally.

When the rice absorbs all the liquid and is soft, the jambalaya is ready to serve. If the rice is cooked and the dish is still a bit liquid, raise the heat until the excess moisture evaporates. If the rice isn't cooked and the dish is dry, add more broth and simmer until it is done.

 Serves: 6 to 8

Japan's hot food eating champion is Morihiro Yamashita, who won a televised contest by eating hot noodles, sushi with extra wasabi, and curried rice spiced with 120 times the usual amount of chile. According to news reports, Yamashita felt faint during the sushi round and in the curry round his tongue went numb and he briefly lost his eyesight—but he eventually won the big, well, chile.

For the Carnivore in Most of Us

A Fired-Up World of Poultry Dishes

Jalapeño-Spiked Chicken Tamales with Tomatillos

Traditionally, lard is used as the fat in making tamales, but vegetable shortening can be substituted. The taste will not be as authentic but the cholesterol will be a lot lower! This tamale filling can also be used to make enchiladas or tacos.

Filling:
- 1 2 1/2- to 3-pound chicken, cut into pieces
- 3 to 4 jalapeño chiles, stems removed, chopped
- 1 medium onion, chopped
- 2 tablespoons vegetable oil
- 1 12-ounce can tomatillos, drained
- 1 cup sour cream
- 3 tablespoons chopped fresh cilantro

Tamales:
- 2 dozen corn husks
- 4 cups dried masa
- 1 teaspoon salt
- 2 1/2 cups chicken broth
- 1/2 cup vegetable shortening

Cover the chicken with water, bring to a boil, reduce the heat, and simmer until the chicken is tender. Allow the chicken to cool and when it can be handled, take it out of the broth. Remove the bones and, using two forks, shred the chicken. Set aside.

Saute the chiles and onion in the oil until softened. Add the tomatillos and simmer for 15 minutes. Add the chicken and simmer for an additional 5 minutes. Set aside. Soak the corn husks in water to soften.

Mix together the masa and salt. Slowly add the broth until the mixture holds together. Whip or beat the shortening until fluffy. Add the masa and continue to beat until fluffy. Drop a teaspoonful of the dough into a glass of cold water and if it floats, it is ready. If it sinks, continue to beat and test until it floats.

To assemble: Select corn husks that measure about 5 by 8 inches. If you don't have husks that wide, overlap two of them and use a little of the masa to "glue" them together. Place 2 tablespoons of the masa in the center and spread the dough thinly and evenly in a 2- by 3-inch rectangle.

Place the chicken and tomatillo sauce down the center of the masa and top with a teaspoon of sour cream and a little of the cilantro. Fold the husk around the masa and filling, being careful not to squeeze. Take two strips of the corn husks and firmly tie each end of the tamale.

Place on a rack in the bottom of a steamer or large pot. Make sure that the rack is high enough to keep the tamales above the water and also high enough to allow a good quantity of water. Place the tamales on the rack, folded side down. If the pot is deep enough, stand them up. Do not pack them tightly in the pot. Cover the tamales with a towel to absorb the moisture. Bring the water to a boil, simmer, and steam the tamales for 2 1/2 hours or until done. To test for doneness, open one end of the husk and if the masa pulls away from the wrapper, it is done.

 Yield: 24

Paprika Chicken (Csirkepaprikás)

Susan Hudgins declares her husband Tom an excellent cook of Hungarian food. Following is his personal recipe for Paprika Chicken, a very refined version of this classic dish. Serve it accompanied by egg noodles, plain rice, or boiled potatoes. In Hungary, this dish is traditionally served with small egg dumplings called galuska.

1 2 1/2- to 3-pound chicken,
   cut into serving pieces
3 tablespoons vegetable oil
2 tablespoons butter or margarine
2 medium onions, chopped
3 large cloves garlic, minced
2 heaping tablespoons mild paprika
1 heaping tablespoon medium-hot paprika
1 tablespoon hot paprika
2 tablespoons brandy
3 cups chicken broth
1 fresh cayenne chile
1/3 cup sour cream
Salt to taste

Brown the chicken in the oil and butter in a large stove-top casserole. Remove the chicken and set aside. Add the onions to the casserole and saute until soft and translucent. Add the garlic and cook for 1 to 2 minutes. Reduce heat to low, stir in the three kinds of paprika, and cook for an additional minute, stirring constantly.

Add the brandy and stir to deglaze the pan. Return the chicken to the pan, add the broth and cayenne. Bring to a boil, reduce the heat, cover, and simmer for 45 to 60 minutes or until the chicken is very tender. Remove the chicken to a serving platter and keep warm.

Bring the liquid in the casserole to a boil and reduce the liquid by 1/3. Stir 1/4 cup of the sauce into the sour cream. Reduce the heat. Slowly stir in the sour cream mixture. Stir until the sauce is smooth and salt to taste.

Pour the sauce over the chicken and serve immediately.

 Serves: 4 to 6

A Maryland company is marketing a product called Squirrel-Away. "Squirrels will fly off bird feeders," says the company's literature, "shaking their heads in disbelief as they head for the nearest bird bath."

The "mystery ingredient" in Squirrel-Away is habanero chile powder, which is mixed with the bird seed. The product is manufactured by American Wild Bird Company, 591 Hungerford Drive, Rockville, MD 20850, but any hot chile powder will work—until the squirrels become chileheads, that is!

As an interesting sidebar to this story, a recent report from the Netherlands tells of Tabasco sauce being mixed with water (one part to 600) and sprayed on crops as a pigeon repellent. Question: were the pigeons repelled by the capsaicin, or by the vinegar?

Zuni Grill's Blue Corn Chicken Taquitos

From the Zuni Grill in Irvine, California comes this New Southwest creation that's a snap to make. Serve these taquitos with a salsa of your choice from Chapter 2.

1 pasilla chile, stem removed
1 small onion, sliced
1 1/2 teaspoons minced garlic
5 tablespoons olive oil
5 Roma tomatoes, chopped
1 cup chicken both
1/2 teaspoon ground cumin
1/2 teaspoon dried oregano
1 bay leaf
1 1/2 pounds skinless chicken breasts
Salt to taste
1 dozen blue corn tortillas
Vegetable oil for deep fat frying

Soak the pasilla in hot water for 15 minutes to soften. Remove the seeds and cut into 1/2-inch julienne strips.

Saute the onion and garlic in 1 tablespoon of the olive oil until soft. Add the chile strips, tomatoes, broth, cumin, oregano, bay leaf, and chicken and simmer, covered, for 35 minutes or until the chicken is very tender and starts to fall off the bone. Strain all the excess juices and either chop or shred the chicken. Salt the chicken to your taste.

Heat the remaining olive oil and soften the tortillas for 10 seconds in the oil. Remove, drain, and dry them with paper towels.

Heat the vegetable oil to 375 degrees.

Place 2 to 3 tablespoons of the chicken filling on a tortilla and tightly roll. Deep-fry for 2 minutes, remove, and drain.

 Serves: 4 to 6

The world's largest ristra—more than 30 feet long—was draped from the courthouse roof to celebrate the Chile and Cheese Festival in Roswell, New Mexico.

A similarly large ristra was fashioned in 1986 by New Mexico State University students—it weighed a half-ton.

Chicken Dilruba

Richard Sterling collected this recipe on an Indian adventure. He decribed it as "a very rich, spicy-sweet chicken dish with distinct Moghul influences. Dilruba means sweetheart. The Moghuls controlled most of India from 1526 until 1839, leaving behind some of India's most famous architecture (the Taj Mahal, for example). The Moghul emperors loved to eat, and twenty-course meals were common in the royal courts. Not surprisingly, Moghul rule had a greater influence on Punjabi cuisine than that of any other conqueror."

2 medium onions, chopped

2 tablespoons chopped ginger

6 tablespoons butter or vegetable oil

3- to 4-pound chicken, skin removed, cut into small serving pieces

1 cup plain yogurt

1/4 cup almonds

1/4 cup walnuts

1/4 cup pumpkin or squash seeds (optional)

1 cup milk

2 tablespoons *garam masala*

1 teaspoon ground turmeric

2 to 3 fresh green cayenne peppers, stems and seeds removed, minced or substitute any small, hot chiles such as serranos or jalapeños

Salt and ground cayenne to taste

A few strands whole saffron, soaked in two tablespoons warm milk

Garnish: Chopped cilantro, whole almonds, whole cashews

Put the onions and ginger into a blender or food processor and process to a smooth paste, about the consistency of applesauce. Heat the butter in a heavy skillet and brown the onion mixture, stirring often.

Add the chicken and yogurt, mix well, and cook over medium heat until the mixture becomes rather dry and the chicken begins to brown. Set aside.

Grind together the almonds, walnuts, and seeds until fine. Stir them into the milk and add to the chicken along with the *garam masala*, turmeric, chile, salt and ground cayenne.

Cook over medium heat, stirring often, until the chicken is very tender and the sauce is very thick, about 10 to 15 minutes. Stir in the saffron mixture and cook for 1 to 2 minutes longer.

Garnish with cilantro and nuts and serve hot.

Serves: 4

Glazed Chicken with Habanero Sauce (Pollo Glazeado con Salsa de Habanero)

From Rodolfo de Garay and Thomas Brown comes this unusual hot and spicy Cuban recipe. It also works well as a barbecue. Make sure the chicken is half-cooked over the coals before beginning to brush on the habanero sauce.

1/2 cup Bitter Orange Juice (see page 11)
1/2 teaspoon freshly ground black pepper
1 teaspoon minced garlic
1 teaspoon salt
4 chicken pieces, such as thighs and legs
1 habanero chile, stem and seeds removed
1 teaspoon lime juice
1 teaspoon white vinegar
2 tablespoons tomato sauce
2 tablespoons grated onion
1/4 cup water
1/4 teaspoon salt
Vegetable oil

Combine the orange juice, black pepper, garlic, and salt to make a sauce (a type of *adobo*) and marinate the chicken for at least two hours, preferably overnight.

Preheat the oven to 400 degrees.

Place the habanero, lime juice, vinegar, tomato sauce, onion, water, and salt in a blender or food processor and blend to make a sauce, adding more water if necessary. Set aside.

Remove the chicken from the *adobo* and reserve the liquid.

Pour the oil in a skillet to a depth of about 1/2 inch. Heat and brown the chicken until golden on both sides. Remove the chicken and place on a baking pan.

Combine the reserved *adobo* sauce with the habanero sauce and brush the chicken pieces with the sauce. Bake for 6 to 10 minutes, turn the chicken, and brush the other side with the sauce. Continue baking for another 6 minutes and repeat until the sauce has been used up and the chicken is done, about 30 minutes.

This dish may be served hot or cold.

 Serves: 4

Note: This recipe requires advance preparation.

Jay's Jamaican Jerk Chicken

Jay Solomon serves up his favorite jerk, chicken. Jay is the author of A Taste of the Tropics *and an expert on Caribbean cuisine. He suggests serving the chicken over rice with fried plantains and okra on the side.*

2 Scotch bonnet chiles, stems and
  seeds removed, minced

6 green onions, sliced

1 medium onion, diced

3/4 cup soy sauce

1/2 cup red wine vinegar

1/4 cup vegetable oil

1/4 cup brown sugar

2 tablespoons fresh thyme

1 teaspoon crushed whole cloves

1 teaspoon coarsely ground
  black peppercorns

1/2 teaspoon ground cloves

1/2 teaspoon ground nutmeg

1/2 teaspoon ground allspice

1/4 teaspoon ground cinnamon

1 1/2 pounds skinless chicken breasts,
  cut into strips

Combine all the ingredients, except the chicken, in a blender or food processor and process for 10 to 15 seconds at high speed to form a marinade. Pour the marinade into a nonreactive bowl, add the chicken, and marinate in the refrigerator for 4 to 6 hours.

Remove the chicken and drain off any excess marinade. Place on a hot oiled grill and cook for 4 to 5 minutes on each side, or until the chicken is done.

 Serves: 4

Note: This recipe requires advance preparation.

Tangy Grilled Chicken

From Shirley Jordan comes this grilled chicken from the island of Grenada. She told us, "Islanders love to cook outdoors. Most cooks in the Caribbean take pride in developing their own spicy marinades. Here is a tangy one that works well for pork as well as chicken."

1 Scotch bonnet or habanero chile, stem
  and seeds removed, finely chopped

1 green bell pepper, stem and seeds
  removed, finely chopped

1 teaspoon dried thyme

1 teaspoon Worcestershire sauce

2 cloves garlic, minced

2 shallots, minced

2 tablespoons butter or margarine

3 tablespoons tomato paste

1/2 cup dry white wine

1/4 cup white wine vinegar

1 chicken, cut in serving-size pieces

Combine the chile, bell pepper, thyme, and Worcestershire sauce and mix well.

Saute the garlic and shallots in the butter until lightly browned. Stir in the tomato paste, wine, and vinegar. Add the chile mixture, bring to a boil, reduce the heat, and simmer for 5 minutes. Allow to cool.

Marinate the chicken in the sauce for 3 to 4 hours in the refrigerator.

Preheat the barbecue. Arrange the chicken on the hot grill and cook, turning pieces often and basting with sauce.

 Serves: 4 to 6

Note: This recipe requires advance preparation.

Pollo en Escabeche Oriental
(Shredded Chicken Yucatan-Style)

From Marta Figel, co-owner of On the Verandah restaurant in North Carolina, comes this Yucatan dish. Why? Because she and her husband vacation there every winter. Marta says this recipe reflects the Spanish influence on the region. She got hooked on this dish at the Los Almedros restaurant both in Ticul and Merida. Serve the chicken with a habanero sauce from Chapter 2.

10 peppercorns

1/4 teaspoon ground oregano

1/2 teaspoon salt

2 cloves garlic, peeled and crushed

1 tablespoon vinegar

2 large red onions, divided

2 heads garlic

Juice of 3 bitter oranges, or substitute 1
  cup Bitter Orange Juice (see page 11)

3 pounds chicken legs and thighs

1 teaspoon salt

1/2 teaspoon ground oregano

1 xcatic chile, stem and seeds removed,
  or substitute yellow wax chile

1 habanero chile, stem and seeds removed

2 serrano chiles, stems
  and seeds removed

Flour tortillas

Place the peppercorns, oregano, and salt in a spice or coffee grinder and grind to a powder. Combine this powder with the garlic and vinegar to make a paste. Set aside.

Preheat the oven to 350 degrees and roast one of the onions and both heads of garlic for 20 minutes. Let cool.

Slice the remaining onion into rings and marinate them in the bitter orange juice. Set aside.

Place the chicken in a stock pot with water to cover (about 3 cups), salt, and oregano, and simmer until the chicken is tender, about 30 minutes. Drain the chicken, reserving the broth, and transfer the chicken to an ovenproof dish. Spread the peppercorn paste over the chicken, sprinkle 2 tablespoons of the bitter orange juice over it, and bake uncovered at 350 degrees until golden brown, about 30 minutes.

Peel the roasted onion and garlic and combine them with the reserved chicken broth. Add the chiles and simmer for 5 minutes. Add the marinated onion rings (strained from the bitter orange juice), bring to a boil, and remove from the heat immediately.

Drain the broth and reserve the broth, chiles, and onions. Separate the chiles from the roasted whole onion and marinated onion rings. Coarsely chop the chiles.

Skin the chicken and shred the meat from the bones. Add the chopped chiles and the whole roasted onion to the chicken and mix well. Reduce the broth by boiling to 1 1/2 cups and add it to the chicken mixture until the mixture is moist but not soupy. Serve with the onion rings.

 Serves: 4

Tajine of Chicken with Lemons and Olives

Rosemary Ogilvie observed: "This dish is probably Morocco's most ubiquitous. However, no matter how often you eat it, you never tire of it, as all chefs put their personal stamp on their creations."

1 3-pound chicken fryer, cut
  in serving pieces

3 tablespoons vegetable oil

1 teaspoon ground ginger

1 teaspoon ground New Mexican red chile

1/2 teaspoon ground turmeric

1/4 teaspoon ground cumin

1/2 cup chopped parsley

1 large onion, thinly sliced

1 tomato, peeled and diced

6 cloves garlic, minced

Juice of 1 lemon

2 cups water

2 lemons, quartered

1 14-ounce jar green olives
  (not stuffed), drained

In a large skillet, quickly brown the chicken in the oil. Add the ginger, chile, turmeric, cumin, parsley, onion, tomato, garlic, lemon juice, and 2 cups of water. Bring to a boil, reduce the heat, and simmer, covered, until the chicken is tender, about 1 1/2 hours, turning the chicken frequently. Remove the chicken from the sauce and keep it warm.When ready to serve, return the chicken to the pan, add the lemon quarters and the olives, and simmer for 10 minutes.

Serve on a plate or in a traditionally made *tajine* with flat, pita-type bread.

 Serves: 4

The chemical commonly called capsaicin not only gives chile peppers their bite, it also may cure cluster headaches, the most excruciating form of headache known. This neurovascular disease, an intense and debilitating pain around one eye, strikes an estimated one percent of the world's population.

A team of reseachers at the University of Florence, Italy, led by Dr. Bruno M. Fusco, treated cluster headache sufferers with a nose spray containing capsaicin for several days. During a 60-day follow-up period, eleven of the sixteen people treated reported a complete cessation of headaches. Two others reported a fifty percent reduction.

The researchers indicated that capsaicin stimulates—then blocks—a class of sensory nerve cells responsible for recognizing and then transmitting pain. One researcher observed that capsaicin "depletes the nerve endings of the chemicals which induce pain." Repeated sprayings, until the burn of the capsaicin could no longer be felt, deadened the nerves and blocked the transmission of cluster headache pain signals to the brain.

Mole Negro Oaxaqueño (Oaxacan Black Mole)

Susana Trilling, who owns Seasons of My Heart Cooking School, told us, "Eliseo, my favorite chile vendor in the largest mercado in Oaxaca, said that there are more than sixty varieties of chiles that are grown only in the state of Oaxaca and nowhere else in Mexico. I have suggested substitutions here to reflect chile varieties more commonly available north of the border. You can use oil instead of lard, but the flavor will change dramatically. In our pueblo, people use turkey, which is traditional, and also add pork meat and a piece of beef to enhance the flavor."

1 whole chicken, cut into serving pieces

6 cups chicken broth

5 chilhuacle negro chiles, stems and seeds removed (save the seeds), or substitute ancho chiles

5 guajillo chiles, stems and seeds removed (save the seeds), or substitute dried red New Mexican chiles

4 pasilla chiles, stems and seeds removed (save the seeds)

4 mulatto chiles, stems and seeds removed (save the seeds), or substitute ancho chiles

2 chipotle chiles, stems and seeds removed (save the seeds)

Lard or oil

1 white onion, quartered

6 cloves garlic

2 tablespoons whole almonds

2 tablespoons shelled and skinned peanuts

2 to 4 tablespoons vegetable oil

2 teaspoons raisins

1 slice of bread (Challah or egg type is best)

1 small ripe plantain, sliced, or substitute a banana

1/2 cup sesame seeds

2 pecan halves

1-inch cinnamon stick

2 whole black peppercorns

2 whole cloves

2 tomatoes, peeled and chopped

5 fresh tomatillos, chopped

1/2 teaspoon dried oregano

1/2 teaspoon dried thyme

1 bar or to taste Mexican chocolate, Ibarra preferred

1 avocado leaf, or substitute bay leaf

Salt to taste

Plenty of fresh tortillas

Simmer the chicken in the broth until tender, about 1/2 hour. Remove the chicken, keep it warm, and reserve the broth.

In a frying pan or comal, toast the chiles, turning once until darkened, but not burned or, as some Oaxaquenas prefer, fry the chiles in lard (or oil). Place in a bowl, cover with hot water, and soak for 1/2 hour to soften. Remove the chiles and place in a blender or food processor and puree, adding a little chile water if necessary to form a paste.

In the same pan, roast the onion and garlic until slightly browned, then remove. Toast the almonds and peanuts slightly and remove. Finally, toast the chile seeds. They should be dark, but not burned.

Heat 2 tablespoons of oil in the skillet and fry the raisins until plumped, remove, and drain on paper towels. Next fry the bread until browned, remove, and drain. Repeat with the plantains. Add more oil if necessary, lower the heat, and fry the sesame seeds slowly, stirring often. When they are slightly browned, add the pecans and brown, remove, and drain the mixture. Save the oil.

Toast the cinnamon, peppercorns, and cloves lightly in a dry pan. Cool and grind in a *mocajete* or spice grinder.

Puree the nuts, bread, sesame seeds and pecans in small batches in a blender or food processor, remove. Add the onions, garlic, plantains and puree, remove. Finally, add the tomatoes and tomatillos and puree.

Heat the remaining oil in a *cazuela* or heavy pot and fry the chile paste, stirring constantly so it will not burn. When it is "dry," add the tomato puree and fry until the liquid has evaporated. Add the ground spices, the nut-bread mixture, the pureed onion mixture, and the oregano and thyme.

Simmer, stirring constantly, and add the chocolate to the mole. Toast the avocado leaf for a second over the open flame and add. Slowly add some of the reserved chicken stock to the mole until the mixture is just thick enough to lightly coat a spoon. Salt to taste.

Continue to simmer for 5 minutes, return the chicken to the mole and heat through. Serve with plenty of sauce and hot tortillas.

Serves: 4 to 6

In the March, 1987 issue of *Albuquerque Living*, editor Rick Homans revealed his "Lifestyle Poll," a survey of the preferences of Albuquerqueans. Here are the results of chile pepper preference questions:

Do you like chile peppers? Yes, 87%; No, 11%.

Do you prefer red or green chile? Green, 47%; Red, 28%.

Which ethnic group prefers red chile? Hispanics, 34%; Anglos, 26%.

Which ethnic group prefers green chile? Anglos, 54%; Hispanics, 31%.

Percentages don't add up to 100 because many people worship red and green chile with equal devotion.

Mole Coloradito Oaxaqueño (Oaxacan Little Red Mole)

Here's another great mole recipe from Susana Trilling. "There are still many señoras in the small pueblos who insist on using their mocaljetes for grinding the ingredients in this celebrated dish."

1 whole chicken, cut into serving pieces

6 cups chicken broth

5 ancho chiles, stems and seeds removed

2 guajillo chiles, stems and seeds removed, or substitute dried red New Mexican chiles

5 whole black peppercorns

5 whole cloves

2 2-inch cinnamon sticks

1 white onion, quartered

10 cloves garlic

3 tablespoons vegetable oil, divided

1 small French roll, sliced

1 small plantain or substitute a banana

2 tablespoons raisins

1/4 cup sesame seeds

10 whole almonds

2 medium tomatoes, peeled and quartered

3 sprigs fresh marjoram or oregano

1 bar or to taste Mexican chocolate, such as Ibarra

1 or 2 avocado leaves or substitute bay leaves

Salt to taste

Simmer the chicken in the stock until tender, about 1/2 hour. Remove the chicken, keep warm, and reserve the stock.

In a large frying pan or *comal*, toast the chiles, turning once until darkened, but not burned. Toast the guajillos a little longer because of their tougher skins. Place the chiles in a bowl and cover with hot water to soak for 1/2 hour to soften. Remove the chiles and place in a blender or food processor and puree, adding a little chile water if necessary, then strain.

Toast the peppercorns, cloves, and cinnamon sticks lightly in a dry pan or *comal*. Cool and grind in a *mocajete* or spice grinder.

In the same pan, roast the onion and garlic cloves until slightly browned. Cool and place in a blender or food processor and puree with a little water.

Heat the oil in the pan until smoking hot and fry the bread until lightly brown, remove and drain on paper towels. Fry the plantain on both sides until browned, remove and drain. Quickly fry the raisins, then remove.

Lower the heat and add the sesame seeds, stirring constantly for a couple of minutes, then add the almonds and continue to fry until both are well browned. Remove and drain.

Put 1/2 of the sesame seeds, bread, plantain, and raisins in a blender or food processor and puree, adding a little water, if necessary, to make a paste.

Wipe out the skillet with a cloth, add 1 tablespoon oil, and heat. Add the tomatoes and fry; remove them, place in the blender, and puree.

Heat another tablespoon of oil in a *cazuela* or heavy pot until almost smoking. Add the chile puree and fry, stirring constantly to keep it from burning. It tends to spatter, so be careful! Fry for a couple of minutes, add the tomato puree, ground spices, and marjoram, and heat through. Stir in the bread mixture and continue to heat, stirring constantly. Add the chocolate and avocado leaves, thin with the reserved chicken stock and continue to simmer for 30 minutes.

Add the chicken, adjust the salt, and heat through. Serve with black beans, rice, and tortillas.

 Serves: 4 to 6

The taste buds and nerve fibers in your mouth are so intertwined that when you eat a hot chile, the chemical pain induced by the capsaicin is perceived as heat by the mouth and brain—and then as pleasure. So reports John Willoughby, a former contributor to *Chile Pepper,* writing in the *New York Times.*

In his article, Willoughby reports that studies by Dr. Barry Green at the Monell Chemical Senses Center in Philadelphia question the contention of chile haters that painful foods such as chiles and raw horseradish act as "gustatory sledgehammers, reducing anything in which they are contained to one dimension by overpowering all other tastes." Dr. Green's experiments with such "masking" showed that this belief is not always true. "Some people were able to taste a variety of flavors after eating hot foods," Willoughby wrote, "but others were not."

But why? One theory from cognitive psychology holds that there are two kinds of people: holistic and analytical. When both eat hot and spicy food, the holistic people might believe that the food is too ridiculously hot to taste anything, while the other group "filters the taste through their analytical sensibility and responds, 'Wow, this is great. I can taste all these incredible strong flavors.'" Dr. Green concluded: "The easiest explanation of why people like pain with their food is simply that it adds a whole new dimension to flavor."

Well, it seems that the pain-loving analyticals are gaining the edge over the holistics—the American Spice Trade Association reported that the consumption of red chile peppers rose by twenty-five percent in 1992. And in a telephone survey of 1,000 people nationwide, conducted by the NRA (no guns—that's the National Restaurant Association), half of the people interviewed said that they liked their food very spicy rather than mildly spicy.

Spicy Chicken Roast
(Murg Naram Garam)

Richard Sterling traveled all the way to Rajastan, India, to collect this recipe. "This makes an excellent Sunday dinner and is also a good camp meal," he noted. "If you put some small potatoes and carrots into the pot with the chicken, it makes a fine, one-dish meal."

3 green onions, chopped

2 tablespoons vegetable oil

12 whole cardamom pods, crushed

1/2 teaspoon cumin seeds

1 teaspoon coriander seeds

8 black peppercorns

3 whole cloves

1 small cinnamon stick

1 teaspoon minced ginger

3 to 4 dried red chiles, such as
New Mexican, stems and seeds
removed, crushed

1 teaspoon sugar

Salt to taste

2 cups water (approximate)

1 whole chicken, cleaned and trussed

Saute the onions in the oil for 2 minutes. Add the cardamom and fry 1 minute more. Stir in all the other seasonings, and heat through. Pour in enough water to barely cover, about 2 cups. Stir well and bring to a boil.

Add the chicken, cover, and reduce the heat. Simmer the chicken for 45 minutes, turning the chicken at least twice. Remove the cover and cook, turning often, until the spice mixture is fairly dry and coats the chicken.

Yield: 4 to 6 servings

According to the *Wall Street Journal*, the city of Guntur, India, may well be the hottest city in the world, even eclipsing cities in the United States and Mexico. The financial newspaper sent reporter Anthony Spaeth to India to check out this claim, and his report was shocking, to say the least.

"In Guntur," he wrote, "salted chiles are eaten for breakfast. Snacks are batter-fried chiles with chile sauce. The town's culinary pride are fruits and vegetables preserved in oil and chile, particularly its karapo pickles: red chiles pickled in chile."

Legend and lore about chiles figure prominently in the culture of Guntur. The people often dream about them, and they believe that hot tempers arise from heavy chile eating and that chiles increase sexual desire. Children begin to eat chile at age five and quickly build up an incredible tolerance.

"Chile is so ingrained in the culture of Guntur that an event like a chile-eating contest would be a silly redundancy," observed Spaeth.

Grilled Chicken Breasts with Peppered Tequila, Citrus, and Cilantro Marinade

Herb expert Lucinda Hutson, author of a book on tequila, provided this recipe. "Spiked with peppered tequila and with the additional fresh flavors of citrus and cilantro, this lively marinade enhances fajitas, steaks, and chicken." She makes her peppered tequila by using one hundred percent agave reposado. The chiles are placed on skewers in the tequila for a few days until the desired heat level is attained.

2 chicken breasts
4 cloves garlic, cut in half
3 tablespoons peppered tequila
3 tablespoons fresh lime juice
3 tablespoons fresh orange juice
1 1/2 teaspoons grated orange zest
1 teaspoon grated lime zest
1/2 teaspoon crushed New Mexican chile
1/2 teaspoon freshly ground black pepper
1 teaspoon brown sugar
3 tablespoons olive oil
3 tablespoons chopped fresh cilantro

Rub the chicken with the garlic and place in a nonreactive dish. Mix the tequila, citrus juices, zest, crushed chile pepper, black pepper, and sugar; add the oil and mix well. Pour over the chicken and add the cilantro. Cover and marinate for two hours or overnight, turning occasionally.

Preheat the oven to 350 degrees.

Remove the chicken and place in a pan. Bake for 20 minutes, basting frequently with the marinade.

 Serves: 2

Note: This recipe requires advance preparation.

Chicken and Goat Cheese Enchiladas with Black Bean Sauce

The versatility of enchiladas is evidenced in this recipe which is served with a sauce made from beans and the more traditional chiles. For something different, leave the beans whole and add to the filling. Use a red chile sauce over the top.

Sauce:

1 cup dried black beans

4 cups chicken broth, or slightly more

1/2 purple onion, chopped

2 cloves garlic, chopped

2 jalapeño chiles, cut in half, stems and seeds removed

2 tablespoons vegetable oil

2 tablespoons dry sherry

1 tablespoon lime juice

2 teaspoons orange zest

Filling:

1 tablespoon ground red New Mexican chile

1 teaspoon garlic powder

1/2 teaspoon ground cumin

1/2 teaspoon dried oregano

1 pound boneless, skinless chicken breasts, cooked and cut into 3/4-inch pieces or shredded

1/2 purple onion, chopped

2 tablespoons vegetable oil

1 medium tomato, chopped

1/2 pound goat cheese, crumbled

1/4 cup chopped fresh cilantro

8 corn tortillas, softened

Garnish: Chopped cilantro, sour cream

To make the sauce: Wash the beans carefully in cold water. Drain them. Soak the beans overnight in 4 cups of the broth. Transfer to a saucepan, bring to a boil, reduce the heat, and simmer for 1 1/2 hours. Saute the onion, garlic, and jalapeño chiles in hot oil in a skillet and add to the beans. Continue to simmer, adding more broth if necessary. When the beans are done, remove them, and drain off some of the liquid. Place the beans, some of the liquid, sherry, lime juice, and zest in a blender or food processor and puree until smooth.

To make the filling: Combine the chile, garlic, cumin, and oregano and toss the chicken in the mixture to coat. Saute the onion in the oil in a skillet. Add the chicken and heat through. Add the tomato and cook for two minutes.

Preheat the oven to 350 degrees.

To assemble: Place some of the chicken mixture on 2 softened tortillas (one on top of the other) on a plate. Sprinkle the cheese and cilantro over the chicken and roll.

Pour some of the sauce over the top of each enchilada and heat for 10 minutes to melt the cheese.

Garnish with additional cilantro and a dollop of sour cream, and serve.

 Serves: 4

Chicken with Dried Orange Peel

From Jim Peyton comes this citrus-infused, spiced-up chicken. Dried orange peel is found in Asian markets. You can substitute fresh orange peel, but be careful not to include the bitter inner white rind.

Marinade:

2 teaspoons cornstarch

2 teaspoons dry vermouth, sherry,
  or white wine

1/2 pound boneless chicken breast,
  cut into 1/2-inch pieces

Sauce:

2 teaspoons minced ginger

2 teaspoons minced garlic

1/2 teaspoon crushed
  Sichuan peppercorns

1 tablespoon dry vermouth, sherry,
  or white wine

3 tablespoons soy sauce

1 tablespoon hot bean sauce

2 tablespoons dried orange peel, soaked
  for 1/2 hour and shredded

2 teaspoons sugar or honey

1/2 teaspoon sesame oil

1 1/2 to 2 tablespoons peanut oil

6 small dried hot chiles such as chile
  de arbol or japones

Combine the ingredients for the marinade; toss with the chicken and marinate for 15 to 30 minutes.

Mix together all the sauce ingredients.

Heat a wok until it is hot and add the oil. When it just begins to smoke, quickly add the chiles and marinated chicken. Stir-fry until the chicken is nearly cooked through.

Add the sauce, cook an additional 30 seconds, and serve with steamed rice.

 Serves: 2

Chef Mark Miller of the Coyote Cafe in Santa Fe has assembled a list of forty-one "Chile Flavor Descriptors," which are divided into the categories of "fruity" and "other" flavors. The fruity flavors included citrusy (particularly orange and lemon), which would apply to most varieties of habaneros and some of the yellow South American ajís, and raisin, which is the ever present aroma of the anchos and pasillas. Other fruity descriptors were black cherry, fig, mango, and melon. In the "other" flavors category, Miller lists chocolate, tobacco, tannic, soapy, green tea, and—how ironic—black pepper.

Pavo Asado with Cranberry Salsa and Cebollas Adovadas

Ahh, Thanksgiving…our favorite holiday, bar none. Crisp fall air. Harvest moons. Family and friends. And food. According to contributor Susan Zamora we should do something different and try grilling—not roasting—our holiday turkey.

- 1 12- to 14-pound turkey, cut in half through the breast and backbone
- 2 tablespoons dried oregano, Mexican preferred
- 4 limes, divided
- Salt and pepper to taste
- 2 bottles of any strong, dark Mexican beer
- 1/2 cup mango juice
- Garnish: Sprigs of cilantro

Prepare a fire of mesquite charcoal in a smoker-grill, or a fire of regular charcoal to which mesquite wood soaked in water is added.

While the charcoal is burning down to coals, flatten the turkey halves slightly and sprinkle them with oregano, the juice of two limes, salt, and pepper.

When the coals are ready, about a half-hour, arrange them in a circle around a small aluminum drip pan filled with 1 bottle of dark beer. Reserve second bottle of beer and add to pan as beer evaporates. Place the turkey halves, breast side up, on the grill 6 to 8 inches above the drip pan. Cover the grill, open the dampers slightly, and smoke the turkey for 45 minutes.

Then open the smoker and baste the turkey with half of the mango juice and, without turning, continue smoking the turkey for approximately 2 more hours. Every half hour, baste the turkey with

the juice of a half of a lime. After the first hour, baste the turkey with the remaining mango juice.

To serve: Transfer the turkey halves to a serving platter and garnish with the sprigs of cilantro. Serve with the Cranberry Salsa and Cebollas Adovado on the side.

Serves: 6

CEBOLLAS ADOVADAS

- 1 1/2 cups water
- 1 cup balsamic vinegar
- 5 tablespoons brown sugar
- 1 teaspoon ground chile de arbol
- 1/4 teaspoon freshly ground black pepper
- 6 medium green onions, cut in half lengthwise with skin left intact

Combine all the ingredients together, except the onions, and mix well.

Pour into a nonreactive pan. Arrange the onion halves, cut side down, in the marinade and refrigerate overnight.

Bake in a 375 degree oven for approximately an hour, or until the onions are glazed and a dark brown.

 Serves: 4

Note: This recipe requires advance preparation.

Cranberry Salsa

2 cups chopped fresh cranberries

1 large orange, peeled and chopped

1 tablespoon chopped cilantro

2 teaspoons grated orange zest

2 teaspoons grated ginger

3 jalapeño chiles, stems removed, chopped

1 tablespoon orange juice concentrate

Combine all the ingredients and allow to sit, while the turkey is cooking, to blend the flavors.

 Yield: 3 cups

"It's horrible to be eaten alive by an animal," said a man who credits a Capsicum spray with saving his life. As reported by Bob Mottram, the outdoors writer for the *Tacoma News Tribune,* Mark Matheny, a general contractor from Bozeman, Montana, and his partner, Dr. Fred Bahnson, were bow hunting for elk in the Gallatin National Forest about 30 miles north of West Yellowstone, Montana. They surprised a female grizzly and her three cubs feasting on a freshly-killed elk and the grizzly mama instantly reacted to protect her cubs.

"She charged with incredible speed," said Matheny. "I had no time to do anything. I held my bow up in front of me for protection, and she just knocked it out of my hand."

The grizzly smashed Matheny to the ground and seized his head in her jaws. Meanwhile, Bahnson had drawn his can of ten percent Capsicum oleoresin spray and charged the bear, screaming at the top of his lungs. The bear turned and was hit directly in the eyes with the caustic spray.

Seemingly oblivious, the grizzly then knocked Bahnson to the ground, turned back to Matheny, and mauled him again. Bahnson recovered and charged the bear again, pointing the can of Capsicum spray at it. He pressed the valve. The can was empty.

The grizzly knocked Bahnson down again, bit him on the arm, and was about to rip out his throat when the spray finally took effect and the bear suddenly broke off the attack, ran back to her cubs and then tore off into the woods.

Matheny suffered from sixteen inches of bear bites on his face and head which required more than 100 stitches to close. But he's okay now, thanks to his partner Dr. Bahnson, who just happens to specialize in facial reconstruction. And thanks to a a certain Capsicum spray, whose brand name remains unknown.

A Fired-Up World of Poultry Dishes

Marinated Roast Turkey with Green Chile Cornbread Stuffing

Chile transforms bland Pilgrims' fare into a festive entree for any holiday feast. The spiciness will be determined by the amount and heat level of the chile used.

Marinade:

   1/4 cup ground red New Mexican chile

   1 cup vegetable oil

   2 tablespoons minced garlic

   1 teaspoon ground cumin

   1/2 teaspoon freshly ground black pepper

   1 10- to 12-pound turkey

Stuffing:

   1 pound sausage, hot and spicy
     variety preferred

   1 large onion, chopped

   1 cup chopped celery

   1 cup chopped green New Mexican chiles

   1 8-ounce package cornbread stuffing mix

   1/2 cup white wine

   1 cup chicken broth

Preheat the oven to 350 degrees.

Combine all the ingredients for the marinade, simmer for 5 minutes, and cool slightly. Rub the marinade over the turkey and inside the cavity. Reserve the remaining marinade.

Brown the sausage and add the onion and celery. Continue to cook until the onion and celery are soft. Remove and place in a bowl. Add the chile, cornbread, wine, and enough of the broth to thoroughly moisten, not saturate, the stuffing.

Stuff the turkey cavity and sew shut. Roast for 20 minutes per pound, basting frequently with the marinade and pan juices.

 Serves: 6 to 8

The medical journal *The Lancet* reported that about 15 to 35 percent of the people who chew nicotine gum to stop smoking become addicted to the gum. Researchers have been experimenting with placebo gums to help nicotine addicts kick the habit that helped them kick the habit.

But there's a catch—finding a substance which imitates the taste and effect of nicotine. After many studies, scientists have developed a nicotine-flavored placebo gum which seems to be working. You may have by now probably figured out where this story is leading, but we'll tell you anyway: capsaicin is the mystery ingredient in this placebo gum—yet another use for this incredibly versatile chemical.

Madras Duck Curry (Vathu Kari)

Arthur Pais and Radhika Radhakrishnan told us, "In the coastal parts of Tamil Nadu in India, this dish is served during major festivals. Although chicken is more popular than duck, the latter is becoming more popular among the middle class and the rich. If you do not like duck, use chicken instead." To enjoy this spicy curry, serve it with plain white rice and a mild vegetable curry.

3 large onions, finely chopped

2 to 3 tablespoons butter or margarine

4 cloves garlic, minced

2 cups coconut milk, divided

1 teaspoon ground turmeric

1 teaspoon ground coriander

1 teaspoon ground cumin

1/2 teaspoon fenugreek

1 teaspoon ground cayenne

1 4-pound duck, skin removed,
cut into serving pieces

1 tablespoon minced ginger

4 serrano chiles, stems and seeds
removed, cut in thin slices

2 dried red New Mexican chiles, stems
and seeds removed, crushed

1 cup diced potatoes

Juice of 1/2 lemon

Salt to taste

Saute the onions in the butter until they are soft. Add the garlic and stir-fry for a minute.

Mix a tablespoon of the coconut milk with the dry spices to make a paste. Add the spice paste to the skillet, stir well, add the duck pieces and continue cooking over low heat for 5 minutes.

Add the rest of the coconut milk, ginger, and chiles, and bring to a boil; reduce the heat and simmer for 15 minutes.

Add the potatoes and continue cooking for another 20 minutes or until the duck is tender. Stir in the lemon juice and serve.

Serves: 4

Researchers at the University of California at San Francisco have been studying atmospheric conditions at Gilroy Foods' Gentry plant in Gilroy, California, to determine if workers who breathe air saturated with chile powder are healthier than those who do not. They recently concluded two types of tests on the employees: breathing capacity and the inhalation of a chile-based breath mist. The study, which is to be concluded by the end of the year, will try to determine if workers who breathe chile-laden air have a higher resistance to colds and allergies.

Chile-Dusted Duck with South-of-the-Border Stuffing

Roast duck with stuffing is as easy to prepare as turkey or chicken. Many people today refuse to consider duck because it is perceived as being extremely fatty. Several simple steps, however, can greatly reduce the fat content. First, if the skin is pricked before cooking, much of the fat will drain off. Second, roast the duck on a rack. Finally, removing the skin before serving will lower the fat content even further.

1 4 1/2- to 5-pound duck, washed
   and patted dry
Salt
5 jalapeño chiles, stems and seeds
   removed, chopped
1 cup diced onion
2 tablespoons butter or margarine
2 cups peeled and chopped
   Granny Smith apples
2 cups 1/2-inch bread cubes
1/2 cup piñon (pine) nuts
1/3 cup chopped cilantro
Ground red chile

Preheat the oven to 325 degrees.

Sprinkle the inside cavity of the duck with the salt.

Saute the jalapeños and onion in the butter until soft. Remove the mixture from the heat and combine with the apples, bread, nuts, and cilantro, tossing gently to mix. Fill the neck and body cavities loosely with stuffing. Skewer the neck shut, cover the opening of the body cavity with aluminum foil, and tie the legs together.

Place the duck on a rack and with a sharp fork, prick the skin at 1-inch intervals, being careful not to prick the meat. This will cause the duck to self-baste continuously so you can put it in the oven and forget it.

Dust the duck with the chile powder and bake for about 3 hours or to an internal temperature of 160 degrees.

 Serves: 4

In another medical advance utilizing capsaicin, researchers at the University of California at San Francisco have discovered that eyedrops containing capsaicin have prevented flare-ups of latent herpes eye infections in mice for up to two months. However, they cautioned the public not to put chile solutions in their eyes because of possible nerve damage and said that more research needs to be done before practical treatments are available.

A Fired-Up World of Poultry Dishes

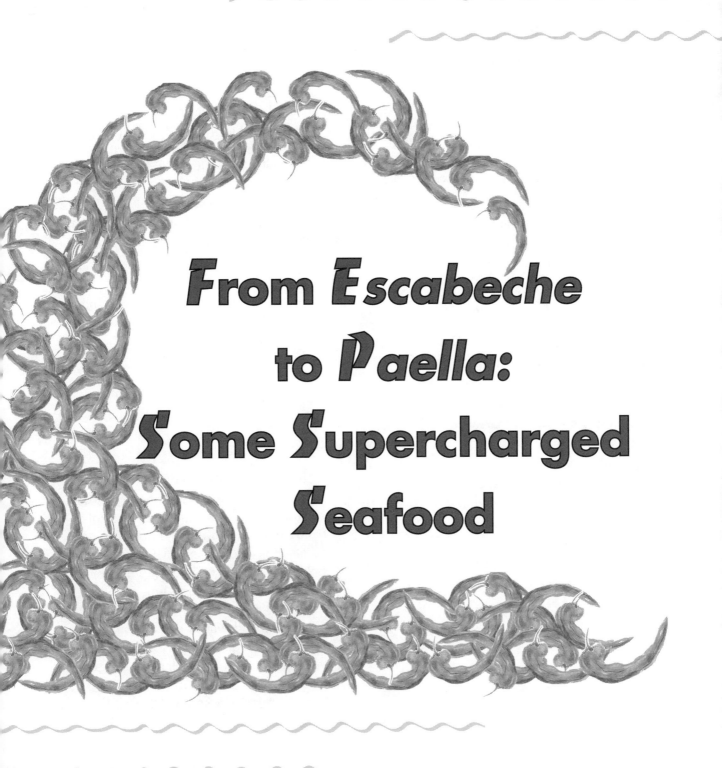

From Escabeche
to Paella:
Some Supercharged
Seafood

Broiled Swordfish with Caribbean Ginger Pepper Sauce

From W.C. Longacre's late, lamented Portside restaurant in Key West comes this intriguing dish. He told us, "From my background in cooking in New Mexico, Hong Kong, and Florida, I invented what I call New-Hong-Key cuisine," he says with tongue firmly in cheek. "It's my combination of the foods of those three regions."

2 tablespoons minced jalapeños
1 teaspoon ground cayenne
2 tablespoons grated ginger
1 tablespoon soy sauce
1 cup water
2 tablespoons cornstarch
1/4 cup lime juice, fresh preferred
1/4 cup unsweetened pineapple juice
1/4 cup sugar
1/4 teaspoon salt
1 tablespoon butter or margarine
Juice of 1 lemon
4 swordfish steaks
1/2 cup pineapple chunks, either fresh,
  or if canned, in their own juice
2 tablespoons dry white wine,
  such as Chardonnay
1 tablespoon chopped cilantro
Cooked white rice

Combine the jalapeños, cayenne, ginger, soy sauce, and 1 cup of water.

In a saucepan, blend the cornstarch, lime and pineapple juice, sugar, and salt until smooth. Bring to a boil. Gradually stir in the jalapeño mixture and simmer until the sauce is thick and transparent. Remove the sauce.

Melt the butter and stir in the lemon juice. Broil the swordfish, basting frequently with lemon butter.

Finish the sauce by stirring in the pineapple chunks, Chardonnay, and cilantro.

To serve, place the fish on a bed of rice and top with a liberal portion of warm sauce.

 Serves: 4

"But for recreation, many of us enjoy whiling away the evening in the 1990s version of a salon—the new or exotic restaurant. And in those restaurants we communally consume hot peppers: It's politically correct thrill-seeking, in which we can publicly engage—on a date, a game of I'll show you mine if you show me yours, and with friends or siblings, open challenge without warfare...It's the dining room equivalent of bungee-jumping."

—Jennifer Farley, *Houston Press*

Fried Snapper with Peppered Lime Salt

Chel Besson, former staff photographer of Chile Pepper, *collected this recipe at the Island Restaurant on Paradise Island in The Bahamas. It uses a common Bahamian condiment, lime salt, which is simply salt combined with minced hot chiles, sprinkled with lime juice, and allowed to dry. The number of people this recipe serves depends upon the size of the fish. Goat peppers are Bahamian relatives of habaneros and Scotch bonnets.*

1 whole small red snapper, cleaned,
  head and tail left on

Juice of 1 lime

1/2 teaspoon freshly ground black pepper

1 teaspoon minced piquin chiles

Lime salt (see above)

1 teaspoon minced goat chiles
  (habanero chiles)

1/4 cup vegetable oil

1 cup water

1 teaspoon minced fresh cayenne chiles

1 small white onion, minced

1 teaspoon ground allspice

Score the snapper in a checkerboard pattern, sprinkle with the lime juice, black pepper, and piquin chiles. Marinate overnight. Remove the fish from the marinade and rub with the lime salt and goat peppers.

Heat the oil in a heavy skillet and add the goat peppers and the fish. Fry the fish until browned, approximately 5 minutes per side. Turn the fish only once during cooking. Remove the fish and keep warm.

Add 1 cup of water to the pan juices along with the cayenne, onion, and allspice. Boil the mixture until thick to form a gravy.

Pour the gravy over the fish and serve.

 Serves: 2

Note: This recipe requires advance preparation.

According to Dr. Villalon of the Texas Agricultural Experiment Station in Weslaco, "As a cash crop, peppers are next only to marijuana in per-acre profit."

Balinese Spiced Snapper
(Ikan Bandeng)

Rosemary Ogilvie collected this recipe in Bali. "This fish makes a truly elegant entree for a dinner party when unwrapped at the table." Tamarind paste, Sambal Oelek, and bamboo leaves are available at Asian and Latin markets.

1 whole snapper or jewfish, about 3 to
    4 pounds, cleaned but head left on

1 medium onion, chopped

2 cloves garlic, minced

1 teaspoon finely chopped ginger

2 tablespoons tamarind paste mixed with
    2 tablespoons of water

1 tablespoon dark soy sauce

1 tablespoon vegetable oil

1 teaspoon ground turmeric

2 teaspoons Sambal Oelek
    (Indonesian chile paste)

1 teaspoon salt

Banana leaves or aluminum foil

3 tablespoons finely chopped cilantro

Bamboo skewers

Preheat the oven to 350 degrees.

Wash the fish, dry well with paper towels, and score the flesh diagonally on each side.

Put the onion, garlic, ginger, tamarind, soy sauce, oil, turmeric, Sambal Oelek, and salt into a blender or food processor and puree until smooth. Rub mixture well into the fish on both sides and put remaining mixture inside the body cavity.

Heat the banana leaves by passing them over the flame of a gas stove to soften. Line a baking dish with 2 or 3 large leaves, or foil. Place fish on the leaves, sprinkle with the cilantro, and fold the leaves over to enclose the fish. Secure with bamboo skewers.

Bake for 35 to 40 minutes. When cooked, the flesh of the fish will appear milky white and be easy to flake with a fork. Fold the leaves back after testing the fish.

Lift the fish onto a serving platter and open the banana leaves.

 Serves: 6

In a 1986 experiment on 20 female volunteers, Leslie Jones, assistant director of the New Mexico Poison Center, has determined that cooking oil works better than water at easing burns caused by capsaicin. During the study, each volunteer placed both hands in peeled, ground green chile for 40 minutes, then placed one hand in cold water and the other in vegetable oil.

During subsequent inverviews, the volunteers indicated that the vegetable oil worked better than water. Jones hinted that perhaps oil works better than water because the capsaicin is oil-soluble but is not immiscible in water. Each year the Poison Center receives over 100 calls from women who suffer burns while processing chile for the freezer, and Jones noted that despite her experiment, the best way to avoid chile burns is to wear rubber gloves.

From Escabeche to Paella: Some Supercharged Seafood

Grilled Bluefish with Chipotle Vinaigrette

This recipe comes from Chris Schlesinger of the East Coast Grill in Cambridge, Massachusetts. He told us, "Here you're talking strength against strength. A very strong, distinct-tasting oily fish versus a hot, smoky, highly acidic vinaigrette. A great combination and both flavors will definitely be heard from. This dish can be served warm or cold—it is a good item for buffets because the cooling-down process doesn't affect the flavors. If you want to make a more colorful presentation, throw a couple of lime halves on the platter and sprinkle with chopped cilantro and raw purple onion."

1/4 cup cider vinegar

1 tablespoon brown prepared mustard

1 tablespoon pureed canned chipotle chile

1 teaspoon chopped fresh cilantro

Juice of 2 limes

1 teaspoon sugar

1/2 cup extra virgin olive oil

Salt and freshly ground black
   pepper to taste

2 8-ounce bluefish filets,
   or substitute mackerel

2 tablespoons vegetable oil

Prepare a charcoal grill.

Whisk the vinegar, mustard, peppers, cilantro, lime juice, and sugar together. Slowly add the olive oil, whisking until well mixed. Add salt and pepper to taste.

Season the fish with salt and pepper and rub with the vegetable oil. Over medium low heat, place the filets skin side up on the grill, and cover them with a pie pan. Cook 10 to 12 minutes, remove the pie pan, turn, and cook an additional 5 minutes. Check for doneness and opacity.

Place the fish on a serving platter, pour the vinaigrette over, and serve.

 Serves: 4

According to *HerbalGram*, the official publication of the Herb Research Association, capsaicin from chile peppers fed to rats along with a 30% saturated fat diet lowered weight gain and triglyceride levels in the liver and blood—good news for victims of clogged arteries.

From Escabeche to Paella: Some Supercharged Seafood

Mixed-Chile Barbecued Halibut with Watermelon Salsa

From chef Peter Zimmer of the Inn of the Anasazi in Santa Fe comes this delicious fish barbecue. Peter was the 1989 winner of the Chefs in America award.

4 chipotle chiles, stems and
   seeds removed

2 cascabel chiles, stems and
   seeds removed

6 ancho chiles, stems and seeds removed

1 medium onion, chopped

4 cloves garlic, chopped

1 tablespoon olive oil

1/4 cup molasses

2 tablespoons honey

3 cups water

1 bunch cilantro, chopped

4 to 6 halibut steaks or filets

Salt to taste

Watermelon Salsa
   (see page 103)

Soak the chiles in hot water for 30 minutes to rehydrate. Remove, drain and pat dry.

Saute the onion and garlic in the oil until soft. Add the chiles and continue to saute for an additional 2 minutes. Add the remaining ingredients (except the halibut, salt, and salsa) and simmer for 10 minutes. Place the mixture in a blender or food processor and puree smooth. Allow the sauce to cool.

Prepare a fire with charcoal or chips.

Dip the halibut in the sauce and grill until done, approximately 2 minutes on each side depending on the thickness of the steaks. Season with salt while cooking.

Serve with Watermelon Chile Salsa and any remaining chile sauce on the side.

 Serves: 4 to 6

A book, *Hunan Hand and Other Ailments: Letters to the New England Journal of Medicine* (Little, Brown) contains two interesting chile pepper maladies: Hunan hand, a painful burning of the fingertips caused by the handling of hot dried chiles, and Jaloproctitis, a burning sensation which occurs during and after—uh, well—elimination of previously eaten jalapeños.

From Escabeche to Paella: Some Supercharged Seafood

Watermelon Salsa

This salsa also goes well with quail or wild game.

8 pasilla chiles, stems and seeds removed

1/4 watermelon, seeds removed, diced

1 purple onion, sliced

1 bunch cilantro, chopped

1/4 cup champagne vinegar

1/4 cup olive oil

3 Roma tomatoes, chopped

Salt and pepper to taste

Cover the pasillas with hot water and allow to sit for 30 minutes to rehydrate. Drain the chiles and cut in thin slivers.

Combine all the ingredients in a nonreactive bowl. Season to taste and chill at least an hour in the refrigerator before serving.

 Serves: 4 to 6

Musician Marshall Crenshaw, quoted in *Rolling Stone* magazine, declares that Bob Dylan has joined the ranks of chile-heads. Crenshaw was asked about rehearsing with Dylan and reported: "He told me to eat hot peppers. He said, 'If you remember to eat hot peppers every day, you'll never get sick.'"

Fish in Ají Sauce
(Escabeche de Pescado)

When Mary Dempsey married a Peruvian she inherited many recipes that she shared with Chile Pepper readers. "As befitting a nation with miles of Pacific coastline, many dishes in Peru use seafood. Escabeche is cold fried fish in a marinade of onion and hot peppers." Serve this fish with sweet potatoes, corn on the cob, and a crisp salad.

4 white fish filets

Flour for dredging

2 tablespoons olive oil

1/4 teaspoon ground cumin

Salt and pepper to taste

6 fresh ají chiles, stems and seeds removed, 4 minced, 2 cut in thin strips, or substitute red serranos or jalapeños

2 cloves garlic, minced

1 medium white onion, cut into thin wedges

1/3 cup white vinegar

Lettuce

Dredge the fish with flour and shake off any excess. Fry the fish in the oil until done. Remove and season with the cumin, salt, and pepper. Set aside to cool.

In the same pan, fry the minced chile and garlic until soft, adding more oil if necessary. Add the onion, chile strips, and vinegar. Simmer for 5 minutes.

Place the fried fish filets on a bed of lettuce and cover with the sauce. Serve warm or at room temperature.

 Serves: 4

From Escabeche to Paella: Some Supercharged Seafood

Paella Mexicana

The Old Mexico Grill in Santa Fe has a marvelous version of this traditional Spanish dish. It is best served over a bed of Mexican rice.

　　3 tablespoons butter

　　12 large shrimp, shelled and deveined

　　2 ounces mussels

　　6 to 8 scallops

　　3 ounces chorizo, sliced and grilled

　　1 cup cooked and shredded chicken

　　1/4 cup chopped red bell pepper

　　1/4 cup chopped green bell pepper

　　1/4 cup chopped yellow bell pepper

　　1/3 cup Salsa Cocida (see page 105)

　　4 ounces clam juice

　　2 cups Mexican Rice (see page 105)

　　2 limes, quartered

Melt the butter and add the shrimp, mussels, and scallops. Saute the mixture for a couple of minutes or until the seafood is half-way done. Add the chorizo, chicken, and bell peppers. Continue to saute for an additional 2 minutes. Add the salsa and clam juice, and cook until the seafood is done and the liquid has been absorbed.

Place the rice in a paella pan, add the seafood mixture, garnish with the limes, and serve.

Yield: 2 servings

Chemists call it a vanillylamide of dicilenic acid; we call it the chemical that makes chiles hot. But now some medical researchers call capsaicin both a cause and potential cure of some forms of cancer. According to one report, capsaicin has been linked to colon cancer through studies conducted among chile pepper eaters in India and Korea. But another study showed that in the liver capsaicin is transformed into a compound that soaks up chemicals called free radicals, which are thought to cause cancer.

"Some of the chemicals in hot peppers appear to be cancer-causing, but the same ones can protect against cancer," said Peter Gannett of the University of Nebraska Medical Center. "The overall effect depends upon how much you eat." Skeptics insist that the researchers are trying to scare us again with another potential carcinogen, just as they have in the past with the highly exaggerated dangers of coffee, sugar, and cranberries.

One critic calculated that a person would have to consume two pounds of capsaicin to see the effects the Nebraska research suggested. Since we can taste capsaicin in solutions as diluted as one part in one million, there may only be two pounds of capsaicin in the entire annual world crop of chiles!

From Escabeche to Paella: Some Supercharged Seafood

SALSA COCIDA

7 tomatoes

6 jalapeños, stems and seeds removed, finely chopped

2 teaspoons oregano

2 cloves garlic, minced

1/2 onion, finely chopped

1 teaspoon white vinegar

1 bunch cilantro, finely chopped

3 tablespoons olive oil

Salt and pepper to taste

Mix all the ingredients together and simmer for 1/2 hour.

 Yield: 4 servings

MEXICAN RICE

1 small potato, peeled and diced

1 carrot, peeled and diced

2 large tomatoes, chopped

1 small onion, chopped

1 cup tomato juice

1 cup peas

3 serrano chiles, stem removed, chopped

1 cup rice, rinsed

2 tablespoons vegetable oil

1 cup chicken broth

Cook the potatoes and carrots until tender. Drain and set aside.

Place the tomatoes, onion, and juice in a blender or food processor and puree until smooth. Remove and add the peas and chiles.

Saute the rice in the oil until brown, being careful that it does not burn. Add the juice mixture and the broth. Bring to a boil, reduce the heat, and cook until done, about 25 minutes.

 Yield: 2 cups

From Escabeche to Paella: Some Supercharged Seafood

Catfish and Lump Crab en Papillote

Amanda Griffin penned an article on Enola Prudhomme's lo-cal Cajun cookery for Chile Pepper *in 1992. This is one of Enola's favorite seafood dishes.*

Parchment paper

Margarine

6 ounces catfish filets

Seasoning salt (1/2 teaspoon ground paprika, 1/4 teaspoon ground white pepper, 1/4 teaspoon ground cayenne, and 1/4 teaspoon garlic powder)

2 drops Louisiana-style hot sauce

3 ounces lump crabmeat

1 tablespoon white wine

2 sprigs fresh dill or 1/2 teaspoon dried dill

1 sprig fresh thyme

3 tablespoons butter

1 lemon twist

Preheat the oven to 375 degrees.

Cut the parchment paper into the shape of a heart and butter it with the margarine. Place the filet on the left side of the heart and dust with the seasoning salt. Sprinkle the hot sauce over the fish and top with the rest of the ingredients.

Fold over the other half of the heart. Starting from one end, crinkle up the edges of the paper, moving toward the other side until completely closed. Be careful to seal tightly. Place on a baking sheet.

Bake until the bag is brown and puffy, approximately 15 to 20 minutes.

 Serves: 2

The debate goes on in the media about the longevity of our love for hot and spicy foods. Writing in *The Miami Herald*, Bob Swift asserts: "Will the next hot new food fad be really hot, as in chile pepper? I fear the answer is yes. Food fads come and go. Sushi came and went. So did blackened redfish. Now, we believe the chile pepper is coming into its own, spreading from the Southwest and Caribbean. Soon, all of us—with the possible exception of devotees of New England boiled dinners—may be burping flames."

Au contraire, counters George Blooston in Savvy magazine. "Is this just another gastronomic fad, destined to shrivel like so many sun-dried tomatoes? If past performance is any guide, the answer is no. Serrano, poblano, habanero, and cayenne peppers, which are native to South America, are the culinary equivalent of kudzu. They take hold of a cuisine and don't let go. The ancients ate them and when the time came, showed them to Columbus, who, you'll recall, set sail in search of a shortcut to India and its enticing spices. It is estimated that today at least three-fourths of the human race takes its meals chile-hot."

Here at the *Chile Pepper* magazine, we take the position that chile peppers have been a fad for at least 9,000 years.

From Escabeche to Paella: Some Supercharged Seafood

Hot Prawn Curry (Erzha Kootu)

"The coast of Tamil Nadu abounds in fantastic seafood but nothing is more desirable than fresh prawns, used in this dry, aromatic curry," wrote Arthur Pais and Radhika Radhakrishnan. *This curry goes very well with plain white rice and mango or coconut chutney. It is also served as a snack with toast. "This dry curry adds zest to beer-drinking sessions,"* the authors added.

2 pounds prawns or jumbo shrimp,
   shelled and deveined

1 tablespoon ground turmeric

Salt to taste

1 tablespoon coriander seeds

1 teaspoon mustard seeds

1 teaspoon fenugreek seeds

6 red New Mexican chiles, stems and
   seeds removed

6 serrano chiles, stems and
   seeds removed

2 medium onions, chopped

2 garlic cloves, chopped

2 teaspoons chopped ginger

3 tablespoons vegetable oil

1/2 cup curry* or cilantro leaves

Sprinkle the prawns with the turmeric and salt, mix well, and set aside.

Roast the coriander, mustard, and fenugreek seeds on a hot griddle until they start to sizzle and pop. Allow them to cool. Place the seeds in a coffee or spice grinder and process them to a powder.

Place the chiles, onions, garlic, and ginger in a blender or food processor and coarsely grind them. Mix with the spice powder.

Heat the oil and fry the mixture of powder and chiles over low heat for 2 minutes. Add the curry leaves and the prawns, mix well, and cook over low heat for 5 or 6 minutes; stir every couple of minutes.

 Serves: 6

*Curry leaves are small, slightly shiny leaves similar in appearance to bay leaves, used in Southeast Asian cooking. There is no substitute.

Sri Lankan Coconut Shrimp

Tina Kanagaratnam, who traveled to Sri Lanka for Chile Pepper, exclaimed: "This is a delightful curry and it's also quick! Firm white fish can be substituted for the shrimp or, although not traditionally Sri Lankan, an equivalent amount of scallops can also be substituted with excellent results."

2 tamarind pods
1/4 cup warm water
2 tablespoons Fish Curry Powder
  (see page 109)
2 tablespoons vegetable oil
1 medium onion, finely chopped
1 teaspoon fennel seeds
1 tablespoon fenugreek
1 large tomato, cut in wedges
1 pound large shrimp, shelled
  and deveined
Juice of 1 lime
1/2 cup coconut milk

Soak the tamarind in 1/4 cup warm water for 20 minutes to soften. Squeeze the softened tamarind pulp with the fingers to extract the juice and strain out any seeds or fibrous matter.

Mix the curry powder with a little water to form a paste.

Heat the oil in a wok and saute the onion, fennel, and fenugreek until the onion is translucent, about 5 minutes. Add the curry powder and continue frying. Add the tamarind water, mix well, and fry for a minute or so longer. Add the tomato wedges and cook until soft, about 10 minutes.

Add the shrimp and lime juice, and cook for 5 minutes more, until the shrimp are almost done. Add coconut milk, stir until thickened, and serve.

Serves: 4 to 6

> Supposedly "hotter than a habanero," the pimenta do cheiro variety of C. chinense from Brazil has been tested by HPLC at New Mexico State University and came up short at a mere 113,000 Scoville Units.

FISH CURRY POWDER

This curry powder can be used for all types of seafood and vegetable curries—fish, prawn, scallops, and eggplant are all possibilities.

>   2 1/4 cups coriander seeds
>   1 tablespoon plus 2 teaspoons
>   fennel seeds
>   1/3 cup cumin seeds
>   1 1/2 teaspoons fenugreek
>   1 tablespoon black peppercorns
>   1/3 cup whole dried red chiles,
>   such as piquins
>   1 tablespoon plus 2 teaspoons
>   ground turmeric

In a dry pan, gently fry, one spice at a time, the coriander, fennel, cumin, fenugreek, peppercorns, and the whole chiles. Fry the chiles until they are dark brown and crispy. Allow the ingredients to cool.

Break the chiles into pieces. Place in a spice or a coffee grinder with the seeds and process to a fine powder. Add the turmeric and mix well.

Store the powder in an airtight container.

Yield: 1 2/3 cups

Firecracker Shrimp

Quick and easy, these shrimp can be grilled or cooked under a broiler. For an outrageously hot version of this recipe, reverse the amounts of cayenne and chile powder.

>   1 tablespoon ground red New
>   Mexican chile
>   1 teaspoon ground cayenne
>   1 teaspoon freshly ground black pepper
>   1/2 cup orange juice
>   1/2 cup flat beer
>   1/2 cup vegetable oil, peanut preferred
>   2 tablespoons brown sugar
>   1 1/2 pounds shrimp,
>   shelled and deveined
>   Skewers

Mix all the ingredients together and marinate the shrimp for 6 to 8 hours in the refrigerator.

Thread the shrimp onto skewers and grill or broil, basting frequently with the marinade.

Serves: 4

Note: This recipe requires advance preparation.

From Escabeche to Paella: Some Supercharged Seafood

Louisiana Shrimp Creole

Jacqueline Brende, who wrote "Some Mumbo Jumbo About Gumbo" for Chile Pepper, *observed: "This dish, reminiscent of French Provençal dishes, is topped with a Spanish sauce—which is the spirit of Creole cooking." Crayfish, lump crabmeat, or chicken can be used in place of the shrimp.*

2 green bell peppers, stems and seeds removed, chopped

3 small onions, chopped

4 cloves garlic, minced

2 tablespoons butter or margarine

6 tomatoes, peeled and chopped

4 teaspoons thyme leaves

4 teaspoons ground cayenne

1 teaspoon ground paprika

3 bay leaves

2 teaspoons freshly ground black pepper

1 teaspoon salt

3 pounds shrimp, shelled and deveined

3 cups cooked rice

Garnish: Chopped parsley

Saute the bell peppers, onions, and garlic in the butter until they become limp. Add the tomatoes and all remaining ingredients, except the shrimp, rice, and garnish. Bring to a boil, reduce the heat, and simmer just long enough to eliminate excess liquid.

Add the shrimp and cook 5 minutes, or until the shrimp just turns pink.

Serve over rice, garnished with the parsley.

 Serves: 6

Hurts So Good, Part 2

Jack Curry, owner of the Prince of Wales Pub in San Mateo, California, insists that his customers sign a release before he'll serve them his Habanero Hamburger. Jack, who's a member of the championship Chili Darters chili cookoff team, begins with a generous one-third pound patty of beef marinated with his Windsor Burger Sauce, made with both fresh and powdered habaneros, then grills the burger and serves it on a large, garnished, and toasted bun.

Those who can finish the burger are awarded a bumper sticker inscribed with the immortal words, "I Survived the Habanero Hamburger." Recordholders of most Habanero Hamburgers consumed at one sitting (five) are Richard "King of the Habaneros" Whiteley and Joe Recto.

"It is said that you can go temporarily deaf after eating an habanero," muses Curry, tongue planted firmly in cheek, "so that you cannot hear your own screams."

From Escabeche to Paella: Some Supercharged Seafood

Pickled Parrot's Seafood Cou-Cou

The Pickled Parrot in Minneapolis used the slogan "The Heat Is On" when serving up this dish, one of chef Mitch Omer's favorite creations.

The Cou-Cou:

1 jalapeño chile, stem and seeds removed, minced

1/4 cup minced green onions

1/2 large purple onion, minced

1/2 large red bell pepper, stem and seeds removed, minced

2 cloves garlic, minced

2 tablespoons stick butter

1 teaspoon kosher salt

1 quart chicken broth

1 1/2 cups white cornmeal

2 cups grated Parmesan cheese

The Seafood Cou-Cou Preparation:

1 teaspoon minced shallots

2 teaspoons minced garlic

2 ounces raw lobster

10 to 12 bay scallops

10 shrimp, shelled and deveined

1 tablespoon unsalted butter

1/2 teaspoon ground Chile de Arbol

1/3 cup heavy cream

2 teaspoons vanilla extract

3 tablespoons coconut rum

2 tablespoons coconut milk

2 tablespoons julienned leek

4 whole crayfish, poached

Saute the jalapeño, green onions, purple onion, bell pepper, and garlic in the butter for about 1 minute; season with salt.

Bring the chicken broth to a boil and gradually add the cornmeal while stirring constantly. Slowly stir in the Parmesan cheese, reduce heat, and cook, stirring constantly, for 20 minutes.

Fold in the sauteed jalapeño mixture and blend well. Pour into a well-greased cookie sheet and refrigerate for at least 5 hours.

Prepare hot coals for grilling.

Saute the shallots, garlic, and seafood pieces in the butter for about 1 minute over high heat. Pour off any excess butter and add the chile, cream, vanilla, coconut rum, and coconut milk. Simmer until slightly thickened and add the leek.

Cut the Cou-Cou into 4 squares 3 inches on a side. Brush the squares with olive oil and grill them until they are heated through, about 1 minute a side, taking care not to burn them.

Top the Cou-Cou with the seafood mixture and garnish each with a crayfish.

Serves: 4

Note: This recipe requires advance preparation.

> "People who like hot peppers are generally more fun to be around. It's an attitude. I can taste all the flavors, through the peppers, even when the food is incendiary."
>
> —Robert McGrath,
> chef of Houston's Sierra restaurant

Hot and Sour Shrimp

This is one of our favorite stir-fries because it is very quick and simple to prepare. To vary the dish, we sometimes add pineapple chunks, bell pepper, green onions, green New Mexican chiles, and/or peanuts.

4 tablespoons rice vinegar

2 tablespoons pineapple juice

1 tablespoon soy sauce

1 tablespoon dry sherry

2 tablespoons catsup

3 tablespoons sugar

1/2 teaspoon ground cinnamon

1/2 teaspoon crushed red
New Mexican chile

2 tablespoons chile oil*

1 tablespoon chopped ginger

1 teaspoon chopped garlic

3/4 pound shrimp, shelled and deveined

1 small onion, cut in wedges
and separated

1 tablespoon cornstarch mixed
with 2 tablespoons water

Combine the vinegar, pineapple juice, soy sauce, sherry, catsup, sugar, cinnamon, and chile to make a sauce.

Heat the oil and stir-fry the ginger and garlic for 10 seconds.

Add the shrimp and stir-fry for about 30 seconds or until they turn pink. Remove and drain.

Stir-fry the onion for 1 minute. Add the sauce ingredients and bring to a boil. Reduce the heat and simmer for 2 minutes. Slowly stir in the cornstarch mixture and continue to simmer until thickened.

Add the shrimp to the sauce, toss to coat, and serve.

 Serves: 2 to 4

*Available in Asian markets.

The fastest-growing fast food chain in Japan is Taco Time, which does not cater to traditional Japanese tastes but boldly advertises its food as the hottest around.

From Escabeche to Paella: Some Supercharged Seafood

Grilled Gulf Seafood with Louisiana Crawfish Sauce

This recipe is from the folks at Charley G's Restaurant in Lafayette, Louisiana, who passed it on to our author, Amanda Griffin. Use whatever commercial seasoning salt (spicy salt) is available for this recipe, or substitute a Cajun spice blend.

The Seafood:

2 teaspoons Dijon mustard

1/2 cup white wine vinegar

1/2 cup white wine

1 tablespoon chopped fresh thyme

1 tablespoon chopped fresh basil

2 tablespoons minced garlic

4 teaspoons seasoning salt

2 tablespoons Louisiana-style hot sauce

2 cups olive oil

2 pounds mixed seafood, shrimp, catfish, black drum, whatever is available in your area

The Louisiana Crawfish Sauce:

1 small onion, chopped

1/2 green bell pepper, stem and seeds removed, chopped

1 celery stalk, chopped

2 to 3 tablespoons butter or margarine

2 teaspoons minced garlic

1 cup shrimp stock

1/4 cup dry white wine

2 teaspoons seasoning salt

2 teaspoons Louisiana-style hot sauce

1 tablespoon white roux*

1/2 pound peeled crawfish tails

1 tablespoon chopped green onions

1 tablespoon chopped parsley

Combine all the ingredients for the seafood, except the oil and seafood, in a blender or food processor and blend for 1 minute. Slowly add the oil until incorporated into the marinade. Marinate the seafood for a maximum of two hours.

Prepare a charcoal grill. Grill the seafood over hot coals, basting frequently with the marinade.

To make the sauce, saute the onion, bell pepper, and celery in the butter for 2 minutes. Add garlic and continue to saute for an additional minute. Stir in the stock, wine, seasoning salt, hot sauce, and roux, and simmer until the sauce thickens. Add the crawfish tails and continue to simmer for 4 minutes. Add the green onions and parsley.

To serve: Place the Louisiana Crawfish Sauce on a plate and top with the grilled seafood.

 Serves 4 to 6

*White roux is made of equal parts of flour and butter or vegetable oil. Heat the oil, add the flour all at once, and cook, stirring constantly, for approximately 5 to 8 minutes, taking care it does not brown.

> "[I like the] excitement...the raw adrenal energy...a kind of hormonal buzz."
> —Robert Del Grande, James Beard Award winner

Fiery Citrus-Cashew Lobster

The cashew nuts add texture to this hot and sweet seafood dish from China. Feel free to substitute shrimp or firm white fish for the lobster. Serve this with rice pilaf and steamed snow peas.

2 teaspoons ground cayenne

3 tablespoons cornstarch

Meat from 3 lobster tails, cut in
  1-inch cubes

1/2 cup orange juice

2 teaspoons rice wine or dry sherry

2 teaspoons rice vinegar

1 teaspoon soy sauce

Vegetable oil for frying

8 small dried red chiles, such as piquin
  or japones

2 teaspoons minced ginger

2 teaspoons orange peel, cut in strips

2 teaspoons cornstarch mixed with
  3 teaspoons water

2 tablespoons toasted cashews

Mix the cayenne and cornstarch together and toss the lobster in the mixture.

Combine the orange juice, wine, vinegar, and soy sauce together in a bowl and set aside.

Heat a wok and add the oil. When hot, add the lobster and stir-fry for a couple of minutes until done. Remove and drain.

Pour off all but 2 tablespoons of the oil. Add the chiles and fry until they start to turn black. Remove and discard. Add the ginger and stir-fry for 15 seconds; then add the orange peel for 15 seconds.

Pour in the orange juice mixture, bring to a boil, and slowly stir in enough of the cornstarch mixture to thicken.

Return the lobster to the sauce, add the cashews, heat, and serve.

Serves: 2 to 4

Frieda's Finest, the California specialty produce company, has introduced Habanero Hearts for Valentine's Day—they're shellacked Habaneros in a heart-shaped wreath in a purple-on-lavender box, complete with a package of dried Habaneros for keeping your Valentine hot.

Kung Pao Scallops

When television cooking star Martin Yan was interviewed by Melissa Stock, he gave her this version of the hot and spicy Chinese classic. "Remember the concept of yin and yang when cooking with chiles. Your meal should be balanced and include sweet foods and hot foods—good contrasts with nothing overpowering."

3/4 pound sea scallops

1 teaspoon sesame oil

2 teaspoons cornstarch

1/4 teaspoon salt

1/8 teaspoon white pepper

1/3 cup chicken broth

3 tablespoons balsamic vinegar
or Chinese dark rice vinegar

2 1/2 tablespoons soy sauce

2 teaspoons Asian chile garlic paste

1 1/2 teaspoons sesame oil

5 teaspoons sugar

3 tablespoons cooking oil, divided

2 teaspoons minced ginger

1 teaspoon minced garlic

6 whole red dried chiles, piquins
or santakas preferred

1 small bell pepper, stems and seeds
removed, cut into 1-inch pieces

1 small onion, cut into 1-inch pieces

2 stalks of celery, thinly sliced diagonally

3/4 cup diced bamboo shoots

1 1/2 teaspoons cornstarch dissolved
in 1 tablespoon water

Cut the scallops in half horizontally. Combine sesame oil, cornstarch, salt, and white pepper. Add the scallops and marinate for 30 minutes.

Combine the broth, vinegar, soy sauce, chili garlic sauce, sesame oil, and sugar in a bowl and set aside.

Heat 2 tablespoons of the oil in a wok on high heat. Add the scallops and stir-fry until they are opaque, or about 2 minutes. Remove the scallops to a bowl and set aside.

Heat the remaining 1 tablespoon of the oil and add the ginger, garlic, and whole chiles, and cook until fragrant. Add the bell pepper, onion, celery, and bamboo shoots. Stir-fry for 30 seconds.

Tip the bowl of scallops slightly and pour juices into the wok. Add the sauce, cover, and cook for 1 minute. Return the scallops to the wok, add the cornstarch mixture, and cook, stirring until the sauce boils and thickens.

Serve over rice.

 Serves: 4

Fred Melton of Jacksonville, Florida, has grown a Jalapeño plant twelve feet, three inches tall that has produced over 1700 pods. The plant was certified for the 1993 Guinness Book of World Records when it was a mere ten feet, six inches tall.

Grilled Scallops with Rocotillo Mango Relish

This Caribbean-inspired dish from contributor Chris Schlesinger features the rocotillo chile, which is not commonly available except in some Latin and West Indian markets. If rocotillos are not available, a rough substitute is one part habanero to six parts ripe pimiento or other mild chile.

1 cup rocotillo chiles, diced

1 small purple onion, diced

1 green bell pepper, stem and seeds
   removed, diced

1 red bell pepper, stem and seeds
   removed, diced

2 ripe mangos, peeled and diced

Juice of 3 oranges

Juice of 4 limes

1/2 cup pineapple juice

1/4 cup chopped cilantro

2 pounds scallops

Salt and freshly ground black
   pepper to taste

Skewers

Combine all the ingredients, except the scallops, and mix well. Blanch the scallops in boiling water for 2 1/2 minutes. Drain and pat dry, and sprinkle with salt and pepper.

Prepare a charcoal fire. Thread scallops on skewers and grill over medium-hot fire until they are golden brown outside and opaque throughout, about 2 to 3 minutes per side.

Make a bed of the relish on each plate and place scallops on top.

 Serves: 4

If you've ever suffered food poisoning from tainted raw oysters, as one of us had (it was a horrendous experience), read on. A team of scientists from the Louisiana State University Medical Center has reported a series of tests on a bacterium, Vibrio vulnificus, found in some raw oysters that causes symptoms ranging from mild diarrhea to dangerous blood poisoning. Some of the suggested oyster treatments ranged from adjusting the storage temperature downward, to heat-shocking them, to zapping them with radiation.

Enter hot sauce. At the American Society for Microbiology meeting last October, the LSU scientists recounted their experiments with test tubes full of oyster bacteria. Ketchup added to the test tubes had little effect. ("That doesn't surprise me," wrote syndicated columnist Calvin Trillin, "When you eat ketchup, you can tell that nothing much is going on.")

Lemon juice worked "moderately well," as did horseradish. But straight hot sauce from a bottle killed all bacteria in one minute flat. Even diluted sixteen to one, the hot sauce killed all the bacteria in five minutes.

"Some of the findings were a little astonishing to us," said Dr. Kenneth Aldridge, one of the researchers. "We had no idea these condiments would be so powerful." They also tested three other varieties of Vibrio bacteria, as well as E. coli, shigella, and salmonella. Hot sauce killed them all.

Hunan Crab and Scallops in Black Bean Sauce

Jim Peyton, one of our contributors, observed: "One fact upon which authorities agree is that the chile-based cuisine of western China is the country's most distinctive and popular." Here is one of Jim's favorite Hunanese chile dishes.

1/2 tablespoon red wine vinegar

1 teaspoon cornstarch

1 1/2 tablespoon dry vermouth, sherry, or white wine

1 tablespoon soy sauce

1/2 teaspoon five-spices powder

1 teaspoon chile oil

3 tablespoons peanut oil, divided

1 green bell pepper, stem and seeds removed, cut into 3/4-inch squares

1 tablespoon minced ginger

3 jalapeño or serrano chiles, stems and seeds removed, minced

1 green onion, minced

1 tablespoon fermented black beans

1/2 pound sea scallops, sliced 1/4 inch thick

1/4 pound fresh crabmeat or substitute imitation crab

2 teaspoons black bean sauce

2 teaspoons sweet bean sauce

Combine the vinegar, cornstarch, vermouth, and soy sauce and mix well.

Heat the wok over high heat, add the chile oil and 1 tablespoon of peanut oil and when it just begins to smoke, add the bell pepper and stir-fry for 30 seconds. Remove the pepper and drain.

Add the remaining peanut oil, heat, and add the ginger, chile, green onion, black beans, scallops, and crabmeat. Stir-fry until the scallops are just cooked through, about 30 seconds.

Return the bell pepper to the wok, add the sauces, and stir-fry for about 30 seconds or until the sauce is slightly thickened. Serve with white rice.

Serves: 2

Vincent's Grilled Lobster with Yellow Hot Chile

One of our favorite restaurants is Vincent Guerithault in Phoenix, where we enjoyed one of the finest New Southwestern meals we have ever experienced. Chef Vincent donated the following recipe to our Hot Spots department.

8 yellow wax hot chiles, stems and seeds removed, chopped fine

2 shallots, chopped fine

1 cup dry white wine

1/2 cup lowfat yogurt

2 teaspoons lemon juice

1 teaspoon tomato paste

1 teaspoon chopped fresh basil

1 teaspoon olive oil, heated

Salt and pepper to taste

4 1-pound lobsters

1 tablespoon olive oil

Combine the chiles, shallots, and wine and bring to a boil. Reduce the mixture until it's almost dry and add the yogurt, lemon juice, tomato paste, and basil. Slowly add the heated oil, and salt and pepper to taste. Heat the sauce but do not allow it to boil.

Cut the lobsters in half lengthwise and remove the stomach and veins. Brush them with olive oil and grill over a very hot fire for 7 to 8 minutes, meat side down first. Turn over for 5 more minutes. Remove and crack open the claws.

Sprinkle the sauce over the lobster and serve.

 Serves: 4

In some cases, capsaicin is indeed a miracle cure. Barbara Conway of Searchmont, Ontario, was suffering from trigeminal neuralgia, a disease caused by damage to the nerve that brings feeling to the face. The facial pain was so agonizing that she would go to a shopping mall, have an attack, and fall down on the floor screaming in agony.

"Suicide crossed my mind a number of times," she said. "I felt that there would never be a cure, and there was no way that I could go on living like this. But then, out of the blue, we stumbled on the odd, unexpected answer."

The odd, unexpected answer to Barbara's agonizing pain was Zostrix, the new medicated capsaicin cream used to deaden the pain of shingles. Under a doctor's direction, she began rubbing the cream on her face every time she felt an attack coming on.

"What I know is that when I use Zostrix, I have no facial pain at all," she said. "I'm not afraid to go to the mall anymore."

Other Hot Entrees: Pastas, Stuffed Chiles, and a Pizza

Jalapeño Pasta

Nanette Blanchard developed this method for making hot and spicy pasta, which has a great fresh chile smell and a golden color with green flecks.

- 6 jalapeño chiles, stems and seeds removed, coarsely chopped
- 3 large eggs, at room temperature
- 2 teaspoons olive oil
- 2 cups unbleached flour
- 2 tablespoons water
- Water or additional flour

Put the jalapeños, eggs, and oil in a blender or food processor and puree. If using a processor, add the flour and continue processing until dough forms a ball. If making the dough by hand, mound the flour on a work surface and make an indentation in the middle of the flour to hold the eggs. Add the egg mixture to the middle of the flour. With a fork, slowly incorporate the flour into the middle of the mixture.

If mixture remains crumbly, add water 1 teaspoon at a time until the dough forms a ball. Knead by hand for several minutes to increase the dough's elasticity.

Using a pasta machine or a rolling pin and a well-floured work area, roll the dough out as thin as possible. Let the sheets of rolled dough dry for about 10 minutes before cutting.

With a sharp knife or a pasta machine, cut the sheets into thin strips to the desired width and hang over a chair back or bar overnight to dry.

To cook, gently immerse the pasta in boiling salted water for several minutes or until tender.

Yield: 3/4 pound

Jalapeño Pasta Omelet

Here is a daring breakfast dish that will delight chile-heads around the country. Feel free to serve it with a salsa from Chapter 2.

- 8 ounces Jalapeño Pasta
- 3 tablespoons extra virgin olive oil, divided
- 1/2 cup chopped green New Mexican chile
- 2 large eggs, beaten
- 3 strips of bacon, cooked and crumbled
- 1 tablespoon chopped fresh cilantro
- Salt and freshly ground black pepper to taste
- 1/2 cup grated Parmesan cheese

Cook the pasta according to the directions. Drain and toss it with 1 tablespoon of the oil. Let it cool completely. You can cook the pasta the night before and store it in the refrigerator until you are ready to use it.

Mix the pasta with the green chile, eggs, bacon, cilantro, salt, and pepper. Heat the oil, pour in the omelet mixture, and lower the temperature. Cook and stir, always in the same direction, until the bottom is evenly browned. Slide the omelet onto a plate, add additional oil if necessary, and return the omelet to the pan to brown the other side.

Serve hot topped with Parmesan cheese.

Serves: 4

Blue Corn Fettuccine with Chorizo and Smoked Chicken in Ancho Chile Sauce

John Sysor of the Spoon River Charcuterie in Charlotte, North Carolina, supplied this recipe. "We smoke our own bacon and chicken, and we make about five kinds of chorizo, including a chorizo borracho, made with Jose Cuervo, that we use in this dish. Any flavorful Mexican-style sausage will be wonderful, however, and smoked turkey can be used in place of the chicken."

10 ancho chiles, stems and seeds removed
1/4 pound smoked slab bacon
1 1/2 cups chopped onions
2 tablespoons chopped garlic
1 teaspoon dried oregano
1/2 teaspoon ground cumin
1/4 cup tequila, optional
3 cups chicken broth or water
1 pound tomatoes
1/2 pound Mexican-style link chorizo
1/2 pound smoked chicken meat,
  chopped or shredded
1 12-ounce package blue corn
  or jalapeño fettuccine
Garnish: 1 1/2 cups grated *queso blanco*
  or Monterey Jack cheese

Place the anchos on a baking sheet in a 200-degree oven for about five minutes until you can smell them roasting. Take care that they do not burn.

Saute the bacon until it renders its fat. Pour off all but a couple of tablespoons of fat, add the onions and garlic, and cook until the onions are soft. Add the oregano and cumin and cook for three minutes, stirring frequently. Stir in the tequila and the broth (or water) and bring to a simmer. Add the chiles, remove from the heat, and steep for five or ten minutes.

Cut the tomatoes in half and roast them cut side down in a heavy skillet over medium heat until blackened.

Place the ancho mixture along with the tomatoes in a blender or food processor and puree until smooth, adding more broth or water, if necessary, to make a sauce. The sauce should be smooth but not too thick. Return to the saucepan and simmer for 1/2 hour.

Add the chorizo, taking care not to boil the sauce. You don't want the sausage to burst. Simmer about 12 to 15 minutes, remove the sausage, slice it, and return it to the sauce along with the smoked chicken. Simmer 5 to 10 minutes more.

Cook the pasta according to manufacturer's instructions, drain, and divide it on four plates. Ladle the sauce on top, garnish with the grated cheese, and serve.

 Serves: 4

Grilled Shrimp with Pasta and Hatch Green Chile Pesto

Here is a recent entree Kip Laramie served up at his Santa Fe Cafe in Rosslyn, Virginia. The restaurant was featured in the Hot Spots department of the magazine.

Marinade:

  1/3 cup chopped jalapeño chiles

  1/3 cup chopped fresh cilantro

  6 cloves garlic

  1/4 cup Worcestershire sauce

  2 1/2 cups olive oil

  1/2 cup fresh lemon juice

  2 pounds shrimp, peeled and deveined

Pesto and Pasta:

  1 cup chopped green New Mexican chiles

  1 cup chopped fresh cilantro

  2/3 cup piñon (pine) nuts

  1/2 cup grated Parmesan or
    Romano cheese

  4 cloves garlic

  1/2 cup extra virgin olive oil

  Salt and pepper to taste

  2 pounds fresh angel hair pasta

Combine all ingredients (except the shrimp) for the marinade in a blender or food processor and mix well. In a nonreactive bowl place the shrimp in the marinade in the refrigerator for 2 hours. Drain the shrimp and grill just before serving.

Place the chiles, cilantro, nuts, cheese, and garlic in a blender or food processor and, while processing, slowly drizzle in the oil to form the pesto. Salt and pepper the pesto to taste.

Boil the angel hair until al dente, being careful not to overcook. Drain the pasta while it is very hot and toss it with the pesto. Top with the grilled shrimp and serve.

 Serves: 6

In September, 1993, chili enthusiasts continued their quest to have chili con carne named "America's Official Food" with a 23-city "Chili Across America" tour featuring a motorized stagecoach with a 300-pound copper chili pot on top.

Southwestern Chile Lasagna

If you like making your own pasta, try substituting blue corn flour for the wheat flour in this recipe. The color and flavor are definitely not Italian!

3/4 pound spicy sausage

1 large onion, chopped

3 cloves garlic, minced

3 large tomatoes, peeled and chopped

1/4 cup tomato paste

2 tablespoons ground red
  New Mexican chile

1 tablespoon chopped cilantro

1/2 teaspoon sugar

1/4 teaspoon dried oregano

Salt and pepper to taste

12 to 14 strips lasagna noodles

2 cups ricotta cheese

1 egg, beaten

6 green New Mexican chiles, roasted,
  peeled, stems and seeds removed,
  cut in strips

1/2 pound provolone cheese, thinly sliced

1/4 cup grated Parmesan cheese

Preheat the oven to 350 degrees.

Crumble and cook the sausage until browned and pour off any excess fat. Add the onion and garlic and continue to saute until the onion is soft.

Add the tomatoes, tomato paste, ground chile, cilantro, sugar, and oregano and bring to a boil. Reduce the heat and simmer for 30 to 45 minutes or until thickened. Salt and pepper the sauce to your taste.

Cook the lasagna noodles until al dente, rinse, and drain.

Combine the ricotta with the egg.

To assemble: Place a layer of noodles in the bottom of a greased baking dish. Top with a layer of the cheese mixture, then the sausage mixture, green chile, and provolone cheese. Cover with a layer of noodles and repeat the procedure, ending with the provolone on top. Top with the grated Parmesan cheese.

Bake for 30 minutes or until thoroughly heated and the cheese has melted. Allow to stand for 10 minutes before cutting.

 Serves: 6

A remedy for bruises in *The Healing Herbs* by Michael Castleman calls for mixing one-half teaspoon of cayenne powder with one cup of warm vegetable oil and rubbing the hot oil onto the bruise several times a day.

Chile Tuna Seashells

This pasta salad makes an excellent entree for a summer luncheon. Try substituting crab or shrimp for the tuna and 1 minced habanero for three of the New Mexican chiles.

- 1/2 pound seashell macaroni
- 1/4 cup mayonnaise
- 2 tablespoons prepared chile sauce
- 2 teaspoons prepared horseradish sauce
- 6 New Mexican green chiles, roasted, peeled, stems and seeds removed, chopped
- 4 green onions, chopped
- 1/4 cup green olives, sliced
- 1 7-ounce can white tuna, drained and flaked
- 1 avocado, peeled, pit removed, chopped

Garnish: Chopped cilantro

Cook the macaroni until al dente. Drain and rinse in cold water.

Combine the mayonnaise, chile sauce, horseradish, and green chiles to make a sauce. Add the onions, olives, and tuna. Allow to sit for 2 hours to blend the flavors.

Gently mix in the avocado, garnish with the cilantro, and serve.

 Serves: 4

Tofu Simmered in Coconut Sauce

From contributor Carrie Brown comes this vegetarian entree. "Canned coconut milk is available in many health food stores and Asian markets. Do not use sweetened coconut cream. Leftover coconut milk should be refrigerated and used quickly. It is excellent in custards, bread puddings, and, of course, curries."

- 1/2 pound tofu, firm variety, drained and cut in 1-inch cubes
- 2 tablespoons vegetable oil, divided
- 1 medium yam or sweet potato, peeled and cut in 1-inch cubes
- 1/2 cup minced onion
- 2 serrano chiles, stems removed, sliced
- 1/2 bell pepper, stem and seeds removed, sliced
- 1 cup coconut milk
- 2 teaspoons dark soy sauce
- 1 teaspoon sugar
- 6 mushrooms, sliced
- 3 tablespoons chopped cilantro

Fry the tofu in 1 tablespoon of the oil until evenly browned. Remove and drain on paper towels.

Heat the remaining oil and brown the yam cubes. Remove and drain.

Add the onion, serranos, and bell pepper. Saute until soft. Stir in the coconut milk, bring to a boil, reduce the heat, and return the yam cubes. Cover and cook about 5 minutes.

Add the soy sauce and sugar. Return the tofu to the skillet and add the mushrooms.

When heated through, add the cilantro, remove from the heat, and serve.

 Serves: 4

Chanterelle Stroganoff

Contributor Wendla McGovern told us, "This is a Russian recipe that I've jazzed up." But do the Russians know about serrano chiles?

1 medium onion, minced
1 clove garlic, minced
1 carrot, peeled and grated
1/4 cup olive oil
1/4 pound fresh chanterelles, thinly sliced
3 1/2 tablespoons whole wheat flour
1 teaspoon dill weed, fresh preferred
1 teaspoon ground nutmeg
1/2 teaspoon ground cayenne
1 green bell pepper, stem and seeds
   removed, minced
2 red serranos, stems removed, sliced
1/4 cup dry white wine
1/2 cup water or vegetable broth
1 cup yogurt, room temperature
1 pound spinach fettuccine
   or other fettuccine, cooked
Garnish: Chopped chives or parsley

Saute the onion, garlic, and carrot in the oil for 10 minutes at medium heat. Increase the heat, add the chanterelles, and cook for 15 minutes, stirring constantly.

Stir in the whole wheat flour and cook for 5 more minutes, stirring constantly. Add the dill, nutmeg, cayenne, bell pepper, and serranos and cook 1 minute more. Gradually add the wine and continue cooking until the sauce has thickened.

Reduce the heat and gradually add the broth. Remove about 1/4 cup of the sauce, mix with the yogurt, and then fold the yogurt mixture into the sauce. Cook a minute or two, stirring constantly.

Serve over fettuccine and garnish with fresh chives or parsley.

Serves: 4

Did capsaicin evolve to protect chile peppers from mammalian predators? That's the theory of Dr. Michael Nee of the New York Botanical Garden. Scientists have long speculated that plants produce secondary metabolites, chemicals that are not required for the primary life support of the plant. These metabolites fight off animal predators and perhaps competing plant species.

In the journal *HerbalGram*, Nee speculates that the capsaicin in chiles may be such a metabolite. It prevents animals from eating the chiles so that they can be consumed by fruit-eating birds who specialize in red fruits with small seeds. Mammals perceive a burning sensation from capsaicin but birds do not. The seeds pass through the birds' digestive tract intact and encased in a perfect natural fertilizer. Experts believe that the wild chiltepin (C. annuum var. aviculare) was spread by this method from South America to what is now the U.S.-Mexico border.

Pizza Marinara Picante

"This is an example of the greatness of simple ingredients in Italian cooking," contributor Natalie Danford wrote us. *"There isn't even any cheese to take away from the spicy tomato flavor."* Prepare the sauce while you are waiting for the dough to rise.

- 1 clove garlic, minced
- 2 tablespoons dried, crushed red chiles, such as pepperoncini or piquin
- 1 tablespoon extra virgin olive oil, divided
- 1 1/2 cups tomato puree
- 1/2 teaspoon salt, divided
- 1 cup water
- 1/2 cup fresh parsley leaves, tightly packed
- 1 recipe Spicy Pizza Dough

Preheat the oven to 500 degrees. If you are using unglazed tiles, place them in the oven to heat up.

Saute the garlic and the chiles in 1/2 of the oil until soft. Stir in the tomato puree, chiles, 1/2 of the salt, and 1 cup water, bring to a simmer, and cook uncovered until thickened, about 40 minutes.

Chop the parsley, combine with the remaining salt and oil, and set aside.

Spread the sauce evenly over the pizza, using the back of a spoon.

Slide the pizza onto the tiles or put the pizza in a pan and bake it in the oven until the crust is brown and crisp, about 10 minutes.

Remove from the oven, sprinkle with the parsley mixture, and serve.

Serves: 2 to 4

SPICY PIZZA DOUGH

- 1/2 cup milk
- 1/2 cup hot water
- 1 package active dry yeast
- 2 tablespoons chile oil
- 2 cups flour
- 2 tablespoons crushed red chiles, such as pepperoncini or piquin
- 1 teaspoon salt

Combine the milk and water and stir in the yeast. Let sit for 5 minutes until foamy and stir in the oil.

Add the flour, chile, and salt and stir to combine. If the dough seems dry, work in more water, 1 teaspoon at a time, until the dough can be formed into a ball. If the dough is too wet, work in additional flour. Knead for 10 minutes on a floured surface until the dough is smooth and elastic but still slightly sticky.

Oil a bowl, place the dough in the bowl, roll it around to coat the dough, and cover with a damp cloth. Let it rise until doubled, about 45 minutes.

Punch down the dough and roll or flatten out the dough to fit the pan, or make a circle if you are placing it directly on the tiles. Poke it a few times with a fork to stop bubbles from forming when it bakes.

Chiles en Nogada

From Jim Peyton, author of El Norte: The Cuisine of Northern Mexico, *comes a classic Mexican recipe from Puebla in central Mexico. He observed: "Chiles en Nogada has infinite variations, mostly related to the fruits in the filling and the types of cheeses used."*

Chiles:

8 poblano chiles, roasted and peeled

2/3 cup minced onion

2 cloves garlic, minced

2 tablespoons vegetable oil

1 1/2 pounds lean ground pork

6 tablespoons raisins

6 tablespoons blanched, slivered almonds

1 1/2 pounds tomatoes, peeled, seeds removed, and chopped

1 cup chopped peaches

1 cup chopped pear or apple

1/4 teaspoon ground cinnamon

1 teaspoon salt

1/2 teaspoon freshly ground black pepper

1/4 cup dry sherry

Sauce (*Nogada*):

1 piece white bread, crust removed

3/4 cup milk, divided

1/2 cup chopped walnuts

1 cup heavy cream

1/3 pound Monterey Jack cheese, grated

2 tablespoons softened cream cheese

1/2 teaspoon ground cinnamon

2 teaspoons sugar

Garnish: Seeds from 1 pomegranate,

2 tablespoons chopped parsley

Make a slit in one side of each chile and carefully remove the seeds.

To make the filling: Saute the onion and garlic in the oil until soft and remove from the pan. Brown the pork in the same skillet, pour off any excess fat, and combine the pork with the onion mixture. Add the remaining ingredients (except the sherry) and simmer, stirring frequently, until most of the liquid has evaporated, about 15 minutes. Stir in the sherry and continue to cook for 5 minutes.

Fill each chile with about 1/4 cup of the filling and place 2 chiles each on 4 serving plates.

To make the sauce, place the bread in 1/4 cup of the milk to soak. Place the nuts, the bread, cream, cheeses, cinnamon, and sugar in a blender or food processor and puree until smooth, adding just enough of the reserved milk to make a thick sauce that is the consistency of a thick milkshake.

Cover the stuffed chiles completely with the sauce and garnish with the pomegranate seeds and parsley. Serve at room temperature.

 Serves: 8

Goat Cheese-Filled Poblanos Rellenos on Black Bean and Sirloin Chile with Chipotle Cream

Rosa Rajkovic, a James Beard Award nominee, gives cooking demonstrations at the National Fiery Foods Show. She is one of Albuquerque's more famous chefs. Here is one of chef Rosa's more complicated creations, but it's well worth the time it takes to prepare it. We have chosen this dish many times because it is so tasty. (Tip: Chilling the rellenos until they are very cold will help the blue corn coating stay crispy after the rellenos are sauteed.)

Chile:

1 pound black beans

1 tablespoon ground cumin

1/4 teaspoon ground cayenne

2 teaspoons paprika

2 ancho chiles, stems and seeds removed

1/4 cup olive oil, divided

1 large purple onion, finely chopped

2 teaspoons finely minced garlic

2 cups peeled, seeds removed, diced plum tomatoes

2 jalapeños, stems and seeds, finely chopped

2 1/2 pounds sirloin, cut in 1-inch cubes

1/4 cup minced cilantro

2 tablespoons minced fresh oregano

2 tablespoons fresh marjoram

Rellenos:

6 large poblano chiles, roasted and peeled

1/2 pound chevre (goat) cheese

1/3 pound cream cheese

1/4 pound blue cheese

2 eggs, beaten

1 cup blue cornmeal

1/2 cup vegetable oil

Chipotle Cream:

1/2 cup sour cream

1/4 cup chevre (goat) cheese

1 small chipotle, (if dry, soak in water first to soften)

Half-and-half or heavy cream

1 tablespoon finely chopped cilantro

To make the chile, rinse the beans, cover with water, and boil for 2 minutes. Turn off the heat and let the beans soak for 2 hours at room temperature.

Toast the cumin, cayenne, and paprika on a dry skillet until they are fragrant, taking care they don't burn. Toast the anchos, cool and place them in a spice or coffee grinder. Process to a fine powder.

Saute the onion in 2 tablespoons of oil until soft and transparent, about 20 minutes. Add the garlic and saute an additional 3 minutes. Add the spice mixture, tomatoes, and jalapeños and saute for about 20 minutes. Add the beans along with the soaking water. You should have enough liquid to cover the beans by 4 inches, adding more water, if necessary. Bring to a simmer and cook, partially covered, for 2 1/2 hours, or until the beans are tender.

Heat the remaining olive oil and saute the sirloin cubes until lightly browned. Add the meat to the beans during the last hour of cooking. Add the cilantro, oregano, and marjoram to the chile 20 minutes before the end of the simmering time.

To make the rellenos, make a slit along one side of a poblano chile and remove the seeds, leaving the stem on.

Mix the three cheeses together and pipe or spoon the mixture into the poblano chiles. Refrigerate until ready to assemble the final dish.

To make the chipotle cream, place the sour cream, goat cheese, and chipotle in a blender or food processor and puree until very smooth, adding enough half-and-half or cream to make the mixture pourable. Add the cilantro and process for a few seconds longer. Pour the cream into a squeeze bottle, but make sure the cilantro is fine enough so it doesn't clog the opening.

Place the beaten eggs and blue cornmeal in two separate, shallow bowls. Heat the oil in a large skillet over medium-low heat. Dip the rellenos in the egg mixture first and then into the blue cornmeal. Saute the rellenos until lightly browned, turning each one three times. Drain on a double thickness of paper towels.

To serve: Spoon the chile into wide soup plates or bowls, top with a relleno, and artistically drizzle the Chipotle Cream over the dish.

Serves: 6

We've been joking about it for years, but now an experimental psychologist at New Mexico Institute of Mining and Technology reports that capsaicin produces a mild form of addiction because it triggers pleasurable endorphins, the body's natural painkillers. According to Dr. Frank Etscorn, "We need a fix of red or green with a side order of endorphins. We get slightly strung out on endorphins, but it's no big deal. It's not like heroin addiction."

Dr. Etscorn, who invented the nicotine patch for treating tobacco addiction, experimented with a new drug called naloxone, which is used to block the effects of a heroin overdose. It also blocks endorphins. To test his theory that capsaicin triggers endorphins, Etscorn fed volunteers jalapeños so hot that "smoke was coming out of their ears." When the burning sensation of the chiles began to subside, Etscorn injected the volunteers with naloxone, and the burning immediately returned, proving that endorphins had been released by the chiles. Etscorn believes that capsaicin has great medical potential for pain reduction.

Breakfast Tacos

This filling can also be used to make a breakfast burrito—just place it in warmed flour tortillas and wrap them up. Whichever way you eat them, they make great breakfast sandwiches.

1/2 cup chopped onion
1 clove garlic, chopped
2 tablespoons butter or margarine
6 eggs, beaten
1/4 teaspoon ground cumin
1/2 cup any salsa
1 cup grated cheddar cheese
8 taco shells
1/2 avocado, sliced

Saute the onion and garlic in the butter until soft. Add the eggs, cumin, and salsa. Scramble the eggs until done.

Remove from the heat and stir in the cheese.

Place the eggs in the taco shells, garnish with the avocado, and serve with additional salsa on the side.

 Serves: 4

Scientists taking ground-temperature measurements at Prudhoe Bay, Alaska, were troubled by foxes who chewed through their instrument cables. According to Dr. Frederick Nelson, who led the project, the scientists wanted to protect their cables without killing or harming the foxes.

Dr. Nelson, writing in the journal *Nature* came up with a solution: "A layer of clear silicone sealant was applied to replacement cables with a caulking gun and distributed evenly with a Tabasco sauce-saturated cloth, and allowed to dry. While the sealant was slightly tacky, pepper sauce was applied liberally to its surface."

The result? "There was no further damage to our instrumentation in two field seasons," Dr. Nelson reports. "No toothmarks penetrated the cables, which demonstrates the effectiveness and tenacity of the pungency of pepper sauce." Dr. Nelson believes that there is great potential for using capsaicin to protect cables and other instruments from what he calls "natural predation."

The pro football game between the Denver Broncos and the San Diego Chargers on December 27, 1987, was played in a blizzard at Denver Stadium. During a discussion of the bitter cold the players had to endure, NBC announcer Jimmy Cefalo discussed a rumor that certain Broncos sprinkled cayenne powder in their socks before the game. According to the story, the cayenne so burned the sweaty feet of the players that they resisted the numbing cold. Cefalo wondered whether the use of cayenne powder was just a locker-room legend?

We wondered: would it work? After all, similar tales tell of hoboes riding the rails while munching on pickled jalapenos to warm up freezing nights. The story may be true—we know that ingesting hot chiles causes gustatory sweating, which cools the body. But since we also know that the topical application of capsaicin can cause severe skin burning—and even blistering in some extreme cases—it makes sense that cayenne could cause a "burning sensation," which might counteract the freezing temperatures.

The major problem with this scenario is that "cold" really means "numb" and "burning sensation" translates as "pain" after a certain point. Although the cayenne might at first give the illusion of heat, it probably would not cause the temperature of the feet to rise significantly, and the resulting pain might be distracting to the player.

It all comes down to this…if time is running out and it's fourth and five to go on your opponent's seven-yard line and you're five points behind, would you rather have your feet numb or in agony?

Incidentally, the Broncos won the game but their hot socks were useless in San Diego during the Super Bowl.

Other Hot Entrees: Pastas, Stuffed Chiles, and a Pizza

Enchiladas Stuffed with Hard-Cooked Eggs (Papadzul)

A unique Yucatecan dish, these enchiladas are traditionally served garnished with a green oil squeezed from toasted pumpkin seeds. This is a very old recipe, reputed to have been served by the Maya to the Spaniards when they arrived in the New World. The legend is possibly true since the name Papadzul *means "food of the lords."*

2 large tomatoes, peeled and chopped

1 habanero chile, stem and seeds removed

2 leaves fresh or 1 tablespoon
   dried epazote*

2 cups chicken broth

1 small onion, chopped

2 tablespoons vegetable oil, divided

1 cup toasted pumpkin seeds,
   finely ground

8 corn tortillas

6 hard-cooked eggs, peeled and chopped

Combine the tomatoes, chile, epazote, and broth in a pan. Bring to a boil and cook for 5 minutes. Remove and strain, saving both the tomatoes and the broth.

Saute the onion in 1/2 of the oil until softened. Add the onion to the tomato mixture in a blender or food processor and puree until smooth. Saute this sauce in the remaining oil for 5 minutes.

Heat the strained tomato broth and slowly stir in the seeds. Simmer until the mixture thickens and is the consistency of thick cream, stirring constantly. Be careful the sauce does not boil or it may curdle.

Dip each tortilla in the warm pumpkin seed sauce to coat and soften it. Place some of the chopped eggs in the center of each tortilla, roll up, and place on a platter. Pour the remaining pumpkin seed sauce over the top, then the tomato sauce, and serve.

 Serves: 4

*Epazote is available in Latin markets or through mail-order sources.

A study conducted by the University of Texas Health Science Center in San Antonio showed that sixty-nine percent of patients tested with Axsain (another capsaicin cream) showed relief from the pain caused by diabetic neuropathy. Axsain is manufactured by GalenPharma, an Illinois-based company which says that 1,000 pounds of jalapeños are required to produce one ounce of the extract used in the cream—which should also be good news for growers.

Other Hot Entrees: Pastas, Stuffed Chiles, and a Pizza

Macedonian Tarte

In regions that were once part of the Ottoman Empire, savory pastries filled with meat, cheese, or vegetables are especially popular. Slices of these pastries, called pite *or* bureki, *can be bought from street vendors or at small cafes known as* bifes (buffets). *They are eaten as snacks throughout the day and are also served as appetizers or main dishes. If fresh red New Mexican chiles are not available, use green ones.*

Pastry:
- 4 cups unbleached white flour
- 1/2 teaspoon salt
- 1/4 pound (1 stick) cold butter
- 2/3 to 1 cup ice water
- 1 teaspoon lemon juice or vinegar
- 1/2 pound (2 sticks) margarine

Topping:
- 1 large onion, cut crosswise very thinly and separated into rings
- 1 tablespoon ground New Mexican chile
- 2 1/2 cups crumbled feta cheese
- 2 green New Mexican chiles, roasted, peeled, stems and seeds removed, cut lengthwise into 1/2-inch-wide strips
- 2 red New Mexican chiles, roasted, peeled, stems and seeds removed, cut lengthwise into 1/2-inch-wide strips

Make the pastry 1 day in advance: Combine the flour and salt. Using a pastry cutter, cut 1/4 pound of the butter into the flour until the mixture resembles coarse bread crumbs. Combine the ice water and lemon juice and add to the flour 1 tablespoon at a time, mixing by hand until all the water is absorbed. Use only enough water to make a stiff dough. Form the dough into a ball, wrap tightly in plastic wrap, and refrigerate overnight.

The next day remove the dough from the refrigerator and let it sit unwrapped for 30 minutes. Knead the margarine by hand, working quickly, until it is softened but still cold.

On a lightly floured surface, roll out the dough until it is very thin. Spread the entire surface of the dough with an even layer of the soft margarine. Starting with the longest edge of the dough, roll the dough into a long fat snake, then coil the snake tightly into a circle. Wrap in plastic and refrigerate for 1 hour.

Preheat the oven to 400 degrees.

Place the dough circle on a floured surface. Do not uncoil the dough. Roll it with a rolling pin as if you were rolling out pie dough. Line a 13 inch-diameter, ungreased, deep-dish pizza pan with the dough, pushing it up to form a 1-inch rim inside the pan.

Cover the top of the pastry completely with the onion rings. Sprinkle the chile powder evenly over the onions. Then crumble the feta cheese over the top. Arrange alternating spokes of red and green peppers on the cheese, radiating out from the center of the tarte.

Bake for 30 to 35 minutes, or until the pastry crust just begins to brown. Remove and slice into wedges like a pizza.

Serve hot or at room temperature.

Yield: 8 large slices

Note: This recipe requires advance preparation.

Hangin' Tree Quiche

"Believe it or not, this is the breakfast that the hang-man of Carson City, Nevada, had every morning during the off season," wrote Bob Kinford. "I stole the recipe from him fair and square and so far he hasn't caught up to me."

- **6 strips bacon**
- **1 8-ounce can or jar of oysters**
- **8 ounces cream cheese**
- **1/2 pint whipping cream**
- **1 cup chopped green New Mexican chiles**
- **1 pie shell**
- **4 eggs, beaten**
- **1/2 cup flour**
- **1/4 teaspoon salt**

Preheat the oven to 375 degrees.

Fry the bacon until crisp, remove it, drain on paper towels, and crumble. Add the oysters to the pan and brown. Remove the oysters from the pan with a slotted spoon and place on a plate. Set the plate aside.

Melt the cream cheese in a microwave or in a double boiler. Whip the cream for 2 minutes, add the melted cream cheese, and whip for an additional 2 minutes.

Spread the bacon, oysters, and chopped chiles evenly over the bottom of the pie shell.

Combine the eggs, flour, salt, cream, and cream cheese mixture, and beat well, 3 minutes by hand or 1 minute in a blender on high.

Pour the batter into the pie shell and bake for 30 to 35 minutes, or until the quiche is lightly browned.

 Serves: 4

Chakchouka

This traditional Tunisian dish could more aptly be called a vegetable hash. There are many versions of this dish, but one ingredient that they all contain is eggs, which are very popular throughout the entire Arab world. This dish can be served as an appetizer or as a light luncheon dish.

- **1 medium onion, thinly sliced**
- **2 cloves garlic, minced**
- **2 tablespoons extra virgin olive oil**
- **4 green New Mexican chiles, roasted, peeled, stems removed, cut in strips**
- **1/4 teaspoon ground cayenne**
- **3 tomatoes, peeled and diced**
- **2 teaspoons white vinegar**
- **1 teaspoon ground cumin**
- **4 eggs**

Saute the onion and garlic in the olive oil until soft. Add all the remaining ingredients, except the eggs, and simmer for a minute.

Make 4 indentations in the mixture and carefully break an egg into each one. Cover and cook over a low heat until the eggs are set.

 Serves: 4

Heat-Seeking
Accompaniments
and Vegetables

Hot South Indian Potato Bonda

This dish, from contributor Linda Lynton, can be described as spicy mashed potatoes fried in a dry coating. The name bonda means "deep-fried potatoes." It is a popular dish throughout India with regional variations. These potato balls can be served as part of a main meal or as a snack.

1 cup all-purpose flour

1 teaspoon rice flour

1/4 teaspoon salt

Vegetable oil for frying, divided

1 to 2 dried red New Mexican
    chiles, crushed

1/2 teaspoon ground mustard

3 to 4 jalapeño or serrano chiles, stems
    removed, minced

1 tablespoon minced ginger

1 large onion, minced

1 pound potatoes, boiled and mashed

1 tablespoon chopped fresh cilantro

1/2 teaspoon salt

Make the coating mix from the flour, rice flour, and salt and set aside.

Heat 1 tablespoon of oil, add the red chile and mustard, and saute for a minute. Add the green chiles, ginger, and onion, and fry until the onion is soft. Remove and mix in the potato, cilantro, and salt. Shape the potato mixture into small balls the size of limes and roll them in the coating mix.

Deep-fry the potato balls in 375-degree oil until crisp and golden.

 Serves: 4

Oven-Roasted Potatoes with Rosemary and Chile

A few years ago, Nancy and her husband, Jeff, were fortunate enough to housesit for a couple in Florence. At their home in the Tuscan hills was a large rosemary bush, and after a month of eating and cooking with rosemary, it became their favorite herb. When Nancy and Jeff returned to New Mexico, they planted some rosemary, which grew into a large bush. Every time Nancy passes by, she runs her hands along the branches, releasing the aroma and remembering Italy. This traditional recipe combines a couple of Nancy's favorites—rosemary and chile.

1/4 cup extra virgin olive oil,
    or substitute a chile oil

3 tablespoons chopped fresh rosemary or
    2 teaspoons dried

2 pounds potatoes, peeled and quartered

2 teaspoons ground chile piquin

Preheat the oven to 350 degrees.

Heat the oil, add the rosemary, and saute for a minute. Pour over the potatoes and toss to coat. Place the potatoes in a roasting pan, sprinkle the chile over the potatoes, and bake for 35 to 40 minutes or until crispy on the outside and soft on the inside.

 Serves: 4

Kabul Party Rice (Birinj Kabuli)

Contributor Arnold Krochmal collected this recipe while stationed in Afghanistan. "This is a special dish prepared for celebrations when guests are expected. If pine nuts aren't available, pistachios can be substituted. The Afghans use lamb tail fat to saute the onions, but since this is not readily available, I suggest butter. This is an excellent side dish with meat, fish or poultry."

1 large carrot, peeled and grated
1 large onion, chopped
2 tablespoons butter or margarine
1 tablespoon chopped serrano chile
1 teaspoon ground cinnamon
1/2 teaspoon ground cardamom
1/2 teaspoon ground cumin
1/4 teaspoon ground cloves
2 1/2 cups cooked white rice
1/2 cup piñon or pine nuts
1/2 cup seedless raisins, rehydrated

Place the carrot in a saucepan and cover with water. Bring to a boil, reduce the heat, and simmer for 5 minutes. Drain and rinse under cold water.

Saute the onion in the butter until lightly brown. Add the chile and fry for an additional minute. Stir in the spices and saute for 30 seconds. Add the carrots and rice, stir in the pine nuts and raisins, and heat through.

 Serves: 6

Yellow Festive Rice (Nasi Kunyit)

We thank Devagi Shanmugan, who runs The Thomson Cooking School in Singapore, for this colorful rice dish that goes well with meat dishes. Remember to use coconut milk, not canned coconut cream, which is too sweet.

20 shallots
3 cloves garlic
2 tablespoons minced ginger
4 teaspoons ground coriander
2 teaspoons ground cumin
1 teaspoon ground turmeric
1/2 teaspoon cayenne powder
1 cup water
2 to 3 tablespoons vegetable oil
6 cups coconut milk
3 cups white rice
4 bulbs lemongrass
Salt to taste

Garnish: Fried green onion rings

Place the shallots, garlic, ginger, coriander, cumin, turmeric, cayenne, and 1 cup of water in a blender or food processor and puree until smooth. Heat the oil until very hot, add the spice paste, and fry until fragrant, about 1 minute.

Add the coconut milk, bring to a boil, reduce the heat, add the rice and lemongrass, cover, and simmer for 40 minutes or until the rice is done. Salt to your taste.

Garnish with the fried green onion rings and serve.

 Serves: 6

Malay-Style Fried Rice
(Nasi Goreng)

This version of fried rice is very different from the more common Chinese fried rice—the addition of pounded chiles makes it a special chilehead treat! Fried potatoes are traditionally used here, but for a healthier alternative, one cubed boiled potato can be substituted.

Chile Paste:

1/2 onion

2 cloves garlic

10 dried red chiles, stems and
   seeds removed

1 teaspoon shrimp paste*

Fried Rice:

1/2 cup vegetable oil

1 large potato, peeled and cubed

1 boneless chicken breast, cubed

8 ounces shrimp, shelled and deveined

4 cups cold cooked long-grain rice

2 eggs

3 large green onions, coarsely chopped

1/4 cup fresh or frozen peas

1 tablespoon soy sauce

Pound the onion, garlic, chiles, and shrimp paste together with a mortar and pestle or puree in a blender or food processor to form a paste.

Heat the oil in a wok to 375 degrees and deep-fry the potato cubes until a crispy golden brown. Remove the potatoes and discard all but one tablespoon of the oil. Add the chicken pieces and stir-fry until white. Remove the chicken. If needed, add a tablespoon of oil and quickly fry the shrimp until they turn pink. Remove and add to the potatoes and chicken.

Stir the cold rice with a fork to separate the grains.

Heat 1 tablespoon of the oil, break the eggs into the wok, and add the green onions. When the eggs begin to set at the edges, scramble them. When the eggs are still semiliquid, add the cold rice, stirring to combine all the ingredients. Add the peas and soy sauce and mix well. Remove the omelette to a separate plate and wipe the wok with a paper towel.

Heat another tablespoon of the oil and fry the chile paste ingredients until fragrant. Add the rice and egg mixture to the chile paste. Add the chicken, shrimp, and potatoes and mix well to combine.

Garnish with the omelette and serve hot or cold, with green chiles in vinegar on the side.

 Serves: 4 to 6

*Shrimp paste is available in Asian or Latin markets.

Peas 'n' Rice

A dish commonly associated with the Caribbean, peas 'n' rice is believed to have originated with the African slaves. Since pigeon peas are grown in just about every backyard in all the islands, it's no wonder they make an appearance at almost every meal. When the dried beans are boiled, the water becomes dark brown and is used to both color and flavor the rice. We were served this dish at almost every dinner we had in the Caribbean, from The Shoal, a popular local Bahamian restaurant, to the Pick-A Dilly Inn and Restaurant, to the Radisson Grand Hotel.

1/4 pound salt pork, chopped
1 tablespoon vegetable oil
1 onion, chopped
1/2 cup chopped green bell pepper
1 stalk celery, chopped
2 fresh tomatoes, chopped
2 tablespoons tomato paste
2 teaspoons thyme
2 cayenne chiles, stems and seeds
 removed, chopped
2 cups rice
1/2 cup pigeon peas, cooked
1 quart chicken broth
Salt and pepper to taste

Fry the salt pork to render the fat. Add the oil, onion, bell pepper, and celery and saute until soft. Stir in the tomatoes, tomato paste, thyme, and chile and simmer for 15 minutes.

Add the rice, cooked peas, and chicken broth. Bring to a boil, reduce the heat, cover, and simmer until the rice is tender and the liquid is absorbed, about 35 minutes. Salt and pepper the peas 'n' rice to your taste.

 Serves: 4 to 6

Capsaicin, the powerful chemical that gives chiles their heat, has been used in yet another medical application—treating the intense pain caused by shingles. Shingles is an eruption of unpleasant skin blisters caused by Herpes zoster, the infamous chicken pox virus.

According to *Prevention* magazine (March, 1988), topically applied capsaicin depletes a neurochemical which carries pain impulses to the brain from nerves in the skin, thus effectively short-circuiting the agony. It is basically the same process which allows the chile lover to adapt to greater and greater amounts of hot chiles.

The treatment for shingles is now available in an over-the-counter cream called Zostrix, which is also being tested for the relief of mastectomy pain and diabetic nerve damage.

Cuban-Style Black Beans

Black beans, the classic Cuban dish, are eaten nearly every day. Most versions are not spicy with chiles, but some cooks like a little heat. This recipe calls for rocotillo chiles, but habanero or your favorite chiles can be substituted. This version may also be pureed and served cold with pepper fritters as a garnish.

7 cups water, divided

1 pound dry black beans

2 bay leaves

1 teaspoon ground cumin

1/4 teaspoon dried oregano

1/4 teaspoon dried thyme

Salt to taste

1/2 teaspoon ground black pepper

1 teaspoon sugar

1 cup chopped onion

2 tablespoons chopped garlic

1 cup chopped cubanelle or
    green bell pepper

1 cup chopped red bell pepper

10 rocotillo chiles, stems and seeds
    removed, chopped, or substitute
    2 habanero chiles

1/4 cup dry sherry

2 to 3 tablespoons extra virgin olive oil

1/4 cup white vinegar

Garnish: Chopped parsley, minced onion

Bring 3 cups of water to a boil, add the beans, bring back to a boil, and boil uncovered for 3 minutes. Turn off the heat and let sit, partially covered, for 1 hour.

Add an additional 4 cups of water, bay leaves, cumin, oregano, thyme, salt and pepper, sugar, onion, garlic, and the chopped green and red peppers. Bring back to a boil, reduce the heat, and simmer for approximately 2 hours. Add the rocotillos and simmer for another 1/2 hour or until done.

Stir in the sherry, olive oil, and vinegar. Garnish with the parsley and minced onion and serve.

 Serves: 8

An inmate at the New Mexico Women's Correctional Facility in Grants lost twelve days of good time for possession of "contraband"—four jalapeños hidden in her prison jumpsuit.

Spiced Indian Lentils

Contributor Barbara Spain commented about this recipe: "Sauteing the cooked lentils with the spices is a technique called 'tempering.' It not only adds extra flavor, but also adds gloss to the finished product."

2 cups lentils

3 cups coconut milk

6 green Thai chiles, stems and seeds removed, chopped, or substitute 3 to 4 jalapeño chiles

1 2-inch cinnamon stick

2 tablespoons chopped onions, divided

2 cloves garlic, chopped

1/4 teaspoon saffron threads

1/2 teaspoon mustard seeds

5 curry leaves (omit if not available)

2 tablespoons vegetable oil

Soak the lentils for 1/2 hour in water, then drain.

Combine the drained lentils with the coconut milk, chiles, cinnamon, half of the onion, garlic, and saffron. Simmer the mixture for 30 to 45 minutes or until the lentils are soft. Remove the cinnamon stick and discard.

Saute the mustard seeds, curry leaves, and reserved onion in the oil for a couple of minutes. Add the lentils and cook for an additional 2 to 3 minutes.

 Serves: 4

Red Beans and Rice

Here is a classic Louisiana recipe. If using a fatty sausage, render some of the fat from the meat first and omit the vegetable oil. Be sure to use red beans rather than kidney beans for this dish.

1 pound dried red beans

1 large onion, chopped

6 cloves garlic, chopped

1 stalk celery, chopped

2 tablespoons vegetable oil

2 tablespoons chopped parsley

1 bay leaf

1 pound tasso, andouille, or other sausage, such as garlic sausage, cut diagonally into 3/4-inch slices

1 1/2 teaspoons ground cayenne

8 cups water

4 cups cooked white rice

Garnish: Chopped parsley

Cover the beans with water and let stand overnight.

Saute the onion, garlic, and celery in the oil until soft. Add the drained beans, parsley, bay leaf, tasso, cayenne, and water. Bring to a boil, lower the heat, and simmer until the beans are soft, about 1 to 2 hours.

As they cook, the beans may start to get creamy. If the beans get soft and the broth is still thin, remove some of the liquid, take a few beans, put them in a sieve, mash them with a wooden spoon, and add back to the beans to thicken broth.

Serve over the rice and garnish with plenty of chopped parsley.

 Serves: 6 to 8

Grilled Zucchini Kebabs

Zucchini works well for these vegetable kebabs, but you can experiment with eggplant, other squashes, even corn on the cob.

4 teaspoons crushed red chile

1/4 cup chile oil

2 tablespoons cider vinegar

1 tablespoon fresh lemon juice

Freshly ground black pepper

2 zucchinis, cut in 1/2-inch slices

1 small purple onion, cut in wedges

16 mushroom caps

Skewers

3 tablespoons Parmesan cheese, grated

Combine the chile peppers, chile oil, vinegar, lemon juice, and pepper. Marinate the zucchini, onion, and mushrooms in the mixture for 1 to 2 hours.

Drain the vegetables and save the marinade. Thread the vegetables on skewers and grill or broil for 12 to 15 minutes, basting frequently with the marinade and turning them often.

When they are just about ready to take off the grill, brush the kebabs with the reserved marinade, sprinkle with the cheese, and grill until the cheese is lightly browned.

 Serves: 4

New Mexico Game and Fish Department officials sentenced five chilehead mule deer to die by firing squad for eating nearly two acres of chile peppers and severely damaging three additional acres. The depradations occurred on the farm of Ben Bouvet in Arrey, just north of Hatch. "The deer there have really taken a liking to the chile," said Lee Duff, Las Cruces supervisor of the department.

Department officers attempted to scare the deer from the field for about a month, but the chile-starved creatures could not control their urges. The executions are regarded by the Animal Humane Association as a last resort when preventative or relocation methods failed. The names of those benefiting from the pre-marinated venison were not made public. No attempt was made to find a "halfway pasture" for the addicted deer.

Southwestern Chipotle Baked Beans

White beans, called haricot beans, include Great Northern, navy, cannellini, white kidney, and small white beans. They are among the most versatile of the common beans. Serve these as a hot replacement for traditional baked beans at your next picnic.

- 3 canned chipotle chiles in adobo, stems removed, chopped
- 1 large onion, chopped
- 2 cloves garlic, chopped
- 1 tablespoon vegetable oil
- 2 teaspoons ground New Mexican chile
- 2 tablespoons adobo sauce, from the canned chiles
- 1/4 pound bacon, cut in 1/2-inch pieces
- 1/2 cup catsup
- 1/2 cup beer or water
- 1/4 cup dark brown sugar
- 1 teaspoon dry mustard
- 3 cups cooked Great Northern beans

Preheat the oven to 325 degrees.

Saute the drained chipotle chiles, onion, and garlic in the oil until soft. Add the chile powder, adobo sauce, bacon, catsup, beer, sugar, and mustard and mix well.

Mix the sauce with the beans and bake for 2 hours or until the beans are tender and coated with the sauce. Add water if the mixture gets too dry.

 Serves: 6

Corn, Squash, and Chile Saute (Calabacitas)

This recipe combines two Native American crops, squash and corn, with chile. One of the most popular dishes in New Mexico, it is also so colorful that it goes well with a variety of foods.

- 3 zucchini squash, cubed
- 1/2 cup chopped onion
- 2 cloves garlic, minced
- 3 tablespoons vegetable oil
- 1/2 cup chopped green New Mexican chile
- 2 cups whole kernel corn
- 1/2 teaspoon dried oregano
- 1 cup grated Monterey Jack cheese

Saute the squash, onion, and garlic in the oil until the squash is tender. Add the chile, corn, oregano, and cheese and simmer for 10 minutes.

 Serves: 4

Chile-Glazed Carrots

The glossy sheen on the carrots is produced when the sugared stock is reduced by cooking. This technique can also be used on other root vegetables such as beets. If extra heat is desired, garnish the carrots with crushed red chile before serving.

- 1 pound carrots, julienne-cut
- 3 teaspoons ground red New Mexican chile
- 3 tablespoons butter or margarine, divided
- 1 tablespoon sugar
- 1 1/2 cups chicken broth

Place the carrots in a single layer in a stainless steel or enamel saucepan. Do not use a cast iron or aluminum pan as it will cause the carrots to discolor.

Add the chile, 2 tablespoons of the butter, and sugar. Cover with the chicken stock. Cover and simmer over medium heat until almost done, about 15 to 20 minutes.

Remove the lid and simmer until the liquid is reduced to a glaze on the vegetables, about 15 to 20 minutes. Shake the pan to coat the carrots and to keep them from sticking. Stir in the remaining butter and serve.

 Serves: 4 to 6

Spiced Cauliflower (Aloo Goby)

Richard Sterling collected this recipe in Rajastan, India. "Cauliflower is one of the most popular vegetables in India. In the northern part of the country it's downright inescapable. Fortunately, no two cooks seem to prepare it in quite the same way. Consider this recipe not as a formula, but as a point of departure."

- 2 teaspoons vegetable oil
- 2 teaspoons sugar
- 1 large cauliflower divided into florets
- 2 onions, sliced and fried
- 2 teaspoons crushed red chile, such as piquin
- 2 large tomatoes, peeled and coarsely chopped
- 1 cup plain yogurt
- 2 teaspoons ground cardamom
- Chopped cilantro
- Salt to taste
- 1/4 cup heavy cream

Heat the oil to low, add the sugar and brown, stirring constantly. Add the cauliflower and mix well to coat with the caramel.

Add the onions, chile, tomatoes, and yogurt, then cover and cook until the cauliflower is tender. Stir in the cardamom and cilantro and cook 5 minutes more. Salt to taste.

Pour the cream over the top and serve.

 Serves: 4 to 6

Cheese and Squash Casserole with Banana Peppers

Here is a tangy dish that can be served as an entree when accompanied by a tomato salad and green vegetable. It can also be used as an accompaniment to a simple roast or grilled meat.

1 medium onion, chopped

2 tablespoons olive oil

2 pounds crookneck squash, sliced
   1/4 to 1/2 inch thick

4 banana peppers, stems and seeds
   removed, chopped

6 Hungarian or yellow wax hot chiles,
   stems and seeds removed, chopped

1/4 cup vermouth

1/2 cup heavy cream

1/4 cup sour cream

1/2 pound Monterey Jack cheese, grated

1 ounce blue cheese

Garnish: 3 tablespoons shelled raw
   sunflower seeds

Preheat the oven to 350 degrees.

Saute the onion in the oil until soft and transparent. Add the squash and peppers and saute until the squash is slightly browned but is still crisp. Remove and set aside.

Pour the vermouth into the pan, raise the heat, and deglaze. Add the heavy cream and simmer until the sauce is reduced by half. Stir in the sour cream.

To assemble: Place some of the pieces of squash in the bottom of a casserole dish. Add a layer of the squash-chile mixture and top with some grated Monterey Jack cheese. Place some more of the sauce on top and continue to layer, ending with a Monterey Jack cheese layer. Crumble the blue cheese over the top. Garnish with sunflower seeds.

Place in oven until heated throughout, about 20 minutes.

 Serves: 4 to 6

Fried Chile Fritters (Molagai Bajji)

"Bajjis, *the Madras version of chiles rellenos, are popular tea-time snacks in Madras and other cities of Tamil Nadu,"* wrote contributor Arthur Pais. *"They are often accompanied by cold coconut or mango chutney. The piping hot* bajjis *and the cold chutney make a terrific combination."*

- 2 cups vegetable oil, divided
- 1/2 cup corn flour
- 1/2 cup rice flour
- 1 teaspoon salt
- 1/2 cup water
- 2 teaspoons ground cumin
- 10 green New Mexican chiles, roasted, peeled, stems on, slit lengthwise on one side

Heat the oil to 375 degrees.

Combine the flours and salt, and add 1 teaspoon of warm oil. Blend in the water to make a thick batter.

Rub the cumin into the slits in the chiles and dip them into the batter.

Deep-fry the chiles for 2 or 3 minutes, until lightly browned.

 Serves: 4

Fiery Citrus Green Beans with Serrano Chiles

These simple sweet and spicy green beans are an excellent accompaniment to roast pork, beef, or lamb as well as poultry and fried fish dishes.

- 4 serrano chiles, stems removed, cut in thin strips
- 1 pound French-cut green beans
- 2 tablespoons orange juice, fresh preferred
- 2 teaspoons orange zest
- 1/4 cup butter or margarine
- 1/4 cup light brown sugar

Combine the chiles, beans, orange juice, and zest. Allow to marinate for an hour.

Melt the butter, add the sugar, and heat until the sugar is dissolved.

Add the bean mixture and simmer until the beans are done and coated with the sauce.

 Serves: 4

Chile-Corn with Cream
(Elote con Crema)

Corn is not the only vegetable that can be used in this recipe; try zucchini, crookneck squash, or even peas.

- 1 small onion, chopped
- 1 clove garlic, minced
- 2 tablespoons margarine or bacon fat
- 2 cups whole kernel corn
- 1/4 cup chopped New Mexican green chile
- 1/2 cup half-and-half
- 1 cup cheddar cheese, cut in cubes

Saute the onion and garlic in the margarine until soft. Add the corn and chile and saute for an additional couple of minutes.

Reduce the heat, add the half-and-half, and simmer until the vegetables are done and the sauce is reduced. Add the cheese and continue to simmer until the cheese melts.

 Serves: 4

Coconut-Orange Rice

This dish is both sweet and hot, complementing both poultry and fish dishes. The rice can be prepared up to the point of adding it to the broth and then held until the party begins. Then the cooking can begin.

- 4 serrano chiles, stems removed, chopped
- 1/2 cup grated coconut, fresh preferred
- 1 1/2 cups long-grain rice
- 2 tablespoons margarine or vegetable oil
- 1 cup orange juice
- 1 tablespoon orange zest
- 2 cups chicken broth
- 3 green onions, chopped, including the greens

Saute the chiles, coconut, and rice in the margarine until the grains turn white or opaque.

Bring the orange juice, zest, and broth to a boil. Add the rice mixture, bring to a boil, reduce the heat, and simmer for 20 minutes or until the rice is done.

 Serves: 6

Just when you thought you had heard of every possible use for capsaicin, along comes Ken Fisher and his Barnacle Ban. This Pittsburgh inventor has received a patent for his formula for mixing epoxy paint and capsicum oleoresin to form a paint that is hated by the mollusks of the world—namely, barnacles, zebra mussels, and tube worms—which will not attach themselves to surfaces of ships and intake valves coated with Barnacle Ban.

The U.S. Navy is now testing Barnacle Ban, which reputedly lasts three or four times longer than the Navy's eighteen-month protection from copper anti-fouling paint—and is much cheaper. Fisher explained how his concoction works: "When barnacles or zebra mussels get on it, they get right off because it attacks the nervous system and sends pain messages." Sore mussels, we guess.

Paprika Mushrooms
(Gombapaprikás)

Sharon Hudgins suggests: "To slice the mushrooms, use a hard-boiled-egg slicer. You'll be surprised how fast and easy it makes the preparation of this dish. In Hungary this dish is served over toasted bread or rolls, or accompanied by dumplings or plain rice. I find that it makes a wonderfully rich side dish to accompany roast chicken or roast pork."

2 medium onions, chopped

3 tablespoons butter or margarine

1 pound fresh mushrooms,
   champignons, or a mixture
   of several kinds of mushrooms,
   thinly sliced

1 large clove garlic, minced

4 teaspoons mild paprika

1 cup sour cream

Salt to taste

Saute the onions in the butter until they are translucent. Add the mushrooms and garlic and stir until well combined and coated with the butter. Reduce the heat to very low, sprinkle the paprika over the mushrooms, and mix well. Cover the skillet and simmer until the mushrooms just begin to turn soft, about 5 minutes.

Just before serving, season with salt and stir in the sour cream. Cook the mixture, stirring constantly, over low heat for 1 to 2 minutes until the sour cream is warm, being careful it does not boil. Serve immediately.

 Serves: 4

Breads and Desserts: Some Hot, Some Not

Beer Biscuits with Hot Beer Cheese Spread

Contributor Rick Lyke selected this recipe from beer-meister Robert Bennett. These are excellent when served with a soup or stew from Chapter 3.

2 1/2 cups all-purpose flour

2 tablespoons sugar

2 teaspoons ground red chile
  such as New Mexican or de Arbol

1 1/2 teaspoons baking powder

1/2 teaspoon baking soda

1/2 teaspoon salt

1/2 cup vegetable shortening

1 tablespoon dry active yeast

2 tablespoons warm water

1/2 cup beer

1/2 cup buttermilk

3 tablespoons melted butter or margarine

Preheat the oven to 400 degrees.

Sift the flour, sugar, chile, baking powder, baking soda, and salt together in a mixing bowl. Cut the shortening into the flour mixture with a fork until all of the shortening is mixed in well with the flour.

Dissolve the yeast into 2 tablespoons of warm water and add to the beer and buttermilk. Add the beer mixture to the flour mixture and mix thoroughly until all lumps are gone.

Place the dough on a lightly floured surface and roll out 1/2 inch thick. Using a biscuit or cookie cutter, cut into biscuits.

Brush with the melted butter and bake for approximately 15 minutes, or until lightly browned.

Serve with Hot Beer Cheese Spread.

 Yield: 15 to 20 biscuits

HOT BEER CHEESE SPREAD

10 ounces sharp cheddar cheese,
  cut in cubes

1/4 cup beer

2 tablespoons Tabasco sauce or your
  favorite Louisiana-style hot sauce

1 teaspoon garlic powder

Place all the ingredients in a food processor or blender and puree until the desired consistency is obtained.

Chile Quiz, Part 2

Q. Consider the following statements:

1. Chiles are more than a fad; they're a way of life.

2. Chiles induce a psychological and perhaps physical dependency.

3. Chiles are dangerous to the uninitiated.

4. Chiles, like avocados, are a cure for gout.

Now, which of the following claims is true about the above statements? (a) 1 and 2, but obviously not 3 and 4; (b) 1 and 4, probably 2, and possibly 3; (c) 3 and—considering current fads—1, but not 2 and 4; (d) possibly 3, 4, and 2, but in all likelihood not 1; (e) 2, 4, and possibly 1, but probably not 3; (f) 1, 2, possibly 3, but not 4; (g) Possibly 1 and 4, but definitely not 2 and 3.

A. We hate these confusing questions—don't you? Correct is (f).initiated.

Blue Corn Chile Bacon Muffins

These muffins need not be served at breakfast only. They complement almost any chili con carne creation, barbecue, or Tex-Mex meal.

- 1 cup all-purpose flour
- 3/4 cup blue cornmeal
- 1/3 cup sugar
- 1 tablespoon baking powder
- 3/4 teaspoon salt
- 1 cup milk
- 1 egg, beaten
- 2 tablespoons melted butter or margarine
- 3 strips crisp bacon, crumbled
- 4 jalapeño chiles, stems and seeds removed, chopped

Preheat the oven to 425 degrees.

Sift all the dry ingredients together.

Combine the milk, egg, butter, bacon, and jalapeños. Add to the dry ingredients and stir to mix.

Lightly grease a muffin pan, fill each well to 3/4 full, and bake for 15 to 20 minutes.

 Yield: 12 to 15 muffins

Chile-Spiced Pumpkin Rolls

These not only go well with a dinner of other chile-infused dishes, but can also replace a sweet roll at breakfast.

- 2/3 cup milk
- 1 package active dry yeast
- 1/4 cup warm water
- 1 cup cooked mashed pumpkin or canned pumpkin
- 1/3 cup brown sugar
- 2 tablespoons orange zest
- 2 tablespoons ground red New Mexican chile
- 1/2 teaspoon salt
- 1/3 cup butter or margarine, softened
- 4 to 5 cups whole wheat flour
- 1 cup raisins

Preheat the oven to 400 degrees.

Scald the milk and allow to cool. Dissolve the yeast in the warm water for 10 minutes.

Combine the pumpkin, sugar, orange zest, chile, salt, and butter and mix well. Add the yeast mixture, 2 cups flour, and raisins. Beat well. Gradually stir in more flour until the dough is stiff enough to be kneaded. Knead on a floured board until the dough is smooth and elastic.

Place in a buttered bowl, cover, and let rise until doubled.

Punch down and turn onto a floured board. Divide into 12 portions. Place into a buttered muffin tin, cover, and let rise until doubled.

Bake for 20 minutes, remove, and brush with butter while hot.

 Yield: 12 rolls

Green Chile Scones

These tender and flaky scones are best served warm from the oven. For entertaining, try cutting scones out with Southwestern cookie cutters such as a saguaro cactus, a chile, or a cowboy boot.

- **2 cups all-purpose flour**
- **1 teaspoon salt**
- **1 tablespoon baking powder**
- **1/3 cup chopped green New Mexican chiles**
- **2 cloves garlic, minced**
- **1 cup plus 2 tablespoons whipping cream, divided**

Preheat the oven to 425 degrees.

Mix together the flour, salt, and baking powder. Add the chiles, garlic, and 1 cup of the cream and stir until a soft dough forms. Place the dough on a floured surface and knead 10 times or until the mixture forms a ball.

Divide the dough into two pieces. Pat each piece out to a 10-inch circle on an ungreased cookie sheet. Brush the top of the dough with the remaining cream.

Bake for 15 minutes or until golden brown. Cut each circle into 8 wedges before serving.

 Yield: 16 scones

Jalapeño Cornbread

You can vary the heat of this bread by decreasing the amount of the jalapeño or by substituting peeled and chopped green chiles. Use blue cornmeal in place of the yellow for a real northern New Mexican specialty.

- **1 cup cornmeal**
- **1 cup all-purpose flour**
- **2 teaspoons sugar**
- **1 teaspoon baking soda**
- **1 teaspoon baking powder**
- **1 teaspoon salt**
- **1/4 teaspoon garlic powder**
- **1 1/2 cups buttermilk**
- **2 tablespoons minced jalapeños**
- **1 cup minced onions**
- **2 eggs, beaten**
- **1 cup grated cheddar cheese**
- **1/2 cup frozen whole kernel corn, thawed**
- **3 tablespoons bacon drippings or shortening**

Preheat the oven to 425 degrees.

Sift all the dry ingredients into a large bowl.

Heat the buttermilk with the jalapeños and onions and let cool.

Combine the buttermilk mixture with the eggs, cheese, and corn. Add to the dry ingredients and mix thoroughly. Add the bacon drippings.

Pour into a greased 9-inch-square pan and bake for 40 to 50 minutes or until the cornbread is golden brown.

 Serves: 6

Tropically Spicy Banana Bread

Lucinda Hutson created this recipe. She is an expert on tequila, which is why peppered tequila appears in this bread—it complements the ginger, tamarind, allspice, and cinnamon. This bread is delicious with cinnamon coffee or a scoop of coconut ice cream.

2 cups all-purpose flour

1 teaspoon baking powder

1/2 teaspoon baking soda

1/4 teaspoon salt

3 tablespoons candied tamarind

2 tablespoons candied ginger

1 teaspoon lime zest

1 1/2 teaspoons orange zest

1 stick butter, softened

1/4 cup brown sugar

1/2 cup white sugar

2 eggs, beaten

1 1/4 cups mashed ripe bananas

1/4 cup orange juice

1/2 teaspoon vanilla

1/2 teaspoon ground cinnamon

1/2 teaspoon ground allspice

3 tablespoons peppered tequila

1/2 cup chopped walnuts

Preheat the oven to 350 degrees.

Sift together the dry ingredients and set aside. Combine the candied fruits and mix with the lime and orange zest.

Cream the butter and the two sugars together and stir in the eggs. Add the bananas, orange juice, vanilla, cinnamon, allspice, and tequila. Stir in the dry ingredients by hand, only enough to moisten all ingredients. Add the candied fruit mixture and nuts.

Pour into a greased loaf pan and bake for 50 to 60 minutes until golden brown.

 Yield: 1 loaf

According to the *New York Times*, one of the foremost celebrity proponents of chile peppers is Zubin Mehta, music director of New York's Philharmonic Orchestra.

"Oh, God, how I love hot food!" Mehta is quoted as saying by Julie Sahni, writing in the *Times*. "I can't go to American restaurants because I feel like I am in a hospital." To avoid problems like being a guest at a dinner of bland food, Mehta carries chiles with him in tiny, jeweled silver boxes.

His reputation for loving fiery foods is so great that other celebrities joke about it. "He's the only person I know," said comedian Alan King, "who puts his own chiles on Mexican food, Indian food, you name it." King also noted: "After dining with him, I don't use a mouthwash, I take Unguentine."

Mehta's favorite chiles are Cayenne, Tabasco, Scotch bonnet, and "Bird" peppers (Chiltepins). It figures, as these are some of the hottest in the world.

European Herb and Cheese Braid

Nanette Blanchard, who wrote about "Kneadful Things" for Chile Pepper, *gave us a hint: "The secret to forming a perfectly braided loaf is to start braiding it in the center and work your way to the ends."*

- 1 tablespoon active dry yeast
- 1/4 cup warm water
- 1 tablespoon sugar
- 3 cups unbleached flour
- 1/2 cup grated Gruyère cheese
- 2 tablespoons grated Parmesan cheese
- 1 1/2 teaspoons salt
- 1/4 teaspoon freshly ground black pepper
- 1 1/2 teaspoons dried oregano
- 1/2 teaspoon dried basil
- 2 tablespoons olive oil
- 2 tablespoons hot pepper sauce
- 1 cup warm water

Topping: 2 tablespoons Gruyère cheese

Dissolve the yeast in warm water for 10 minutes.

Stir in the sugar, flour, cheeses, salt, black pepper, oregano, and basil. Mix the oil, hot pepper sauce, and the water together. Slowly add to the dry mixture and blend all the ingredients.

Turn the dough out onto a floured board and knead until it is smooth and satiny, about 10 to 15 minutes.

Oil a bowl and turn the dough in the bowl to cover with the oil and let rise for 1 1/2 hours or until it has doubled in bulk.

Divide the dough into three pieces and roll each piece into a 15-inch log. Braid, starting from the center, and tuck the ends under. Place on a greased baking sheet and cover with plastic wrap. Let it rise in a warm place for 45 minutes or until almost doubled in bulk.

While waiting for the braided dough to rise, preheat the oven to 375 degrees.

Bake the bread for 25 to 30 minutes or until it is golden brown and sounds hollow when tapped on the bottom. Remove from the oven and sprinkle the Gruyère cheese on the top.

 Yield: 1 loaf

According to L.M. Boyd, writing in the *Austin American-Statesman*, several manufacturers of dandruff shampoo have added capsaicin to their formulas to provide the extra "tingle" that gives the illusion that the product is working.

Ethiopian Ambasha

This fiery-sweet spice bread, also from Nanette Blanchard, is baked in a pizza pan. Several Ethiopian breads incorporate berbere, *which is a hot pepper seasoning, either mixed in the actual bread dough or spread on top as in this recipe. This simplified version uses a quick substitute, but any* berbere *seasoning can be substituted.*

1 tablespoon active dry yeast

1/4 cup warm water (about 110 degrees)

2 tablespoons ground coriander

1 teaspoon ground cardamom

1/2 teaspoon white pepper

1 teaspoon ground fenugreek

2 teaspoons salt

1/3 cup vegetable oil

1 1/4 cups lukewarm water

5 cups unbleached flour

Topping:

1 tablespoon ground hot red chile,
    such as cayenne or piquin

2 tablespoons oil

1/4 teaspoon ground ginger

Pinch of ground cloves

1/8 teaspoon ground cinnamon

Dissolve the yeast in the warm water for 10 minutes. Add the coriander, cardamom, white pepper, fenugreek, salt, oil, and lukewarm water and stir well. Slowly add the flour until a ball of dough is formed.

On a floured board, knead the dough for 10 minutes or until it is smooth and tiny bubbles form. Note: This recipe makes a stickier dough than usual.

Pinch off a 1-inch round of dough. With floured hands, spread the dough out on an ungreased pizza pan. Using a sharp knife, score the dough in a design similar to the spokes of a bicycle wheel. Place the reserved ball of dough in the center of the scored dough. Cover and let rise for 1 hour.

While waiting for the dough to rise, preheat the oven to 350 degrees.

Bake for 1 hour or until golden brown.

Combine the topping ingredients and, while the bread is still warm, brush with the topping.

 Yield: 1 loaf

Note: Nanette Blanchard does not recommend that you make this bread in a food processor.

Creme de Menthe Natillas

Natillas, a soft custard pudding, is a traditional New Mexican holiday dessert made with cinnamon. We add Crème de Menthe for a cool minty taste to complement the chile dishes we serve.

- 4 eggs, separated
- 4 tablespoons flour
- 4 cups whole milk, divided
- 3/4 cup sugar
- 1 tablespoon Crème de Menthe liqueur

Combine the egg yolks, flour, and 1 cup of milk and beat to form a smooth paste.

Combine the remaining milk and sugar and heat to scalding. Add the egg mixture and continue to cook, on medium heat, stirring until thickened to a soft custard consistency.

Remove from the heat, allow to cool, and stir in the liqueur.

Beat the egg whites until they are stiff but not dry. Gently fold them into the custard and dish up into individual bowls.

The pudding can be chilled or served warm.

 Serves: 6 to 8

Toasted Chile Custard

From Fourth Street Grill in Berkeley, California, came this hot and spicy dessert, which appeared in an early issue of Chile Pepper.

- 2 eggs
- 2 egg yolks
- 1/3 cup brown sugar, plus approximately 1/8 cup more
- 1/4 teaspoon salt
- 2 cups cream
- 1/4 teaspoon vanilla
- 1 teaspoon ground chile de Arbol

Preheat the oven to 300 degrees.

Whisk the eggs and egg yolks with 1/3 cup brown sugar and the salt until just mixed.

Scald the cream and add the vanilla. Add half the scalded cream to the egg mixture, stirring constantly. Add the egg mixture back into the rest of the cream in the pan and cook over low heat, stirring constantly until the custard coats the spoon.

Pour into four 4-ounce ramekins (small baking dishes), place in a pan of water (1 inch deep), and bake for 35 minutes. Remove from the oven and cool for 3 hours in the refrigerator.

When ready to serve: Sprinkle approximately 1/4 teaspoon of chile powder over the top of each custard and then top with a thin layer of sifted brown sugar. Place under a broiler until the sugar is melted but not burned. Serve immediately.

 Serves: 4

White Chocolate Ancho Chile Ice Cream

From Suzy Dayton, the pastry chef at the famed Coyote Cafe in Santa Fe, comes a considerably milder ice cream than the preceding recipe made with chiltepins.

  3 ancho chiles, stems removed
  1/2 teaspoon ground cinnamon
  1/4 teaspoon ground cloves
  6 ounces (2 bars) good quality white
     chocolate such as Tobler or Lindt
  2 cups heavy cream
  2 cups milk
  3/4 cup sugar
  1 vanilla bean
  6 egg yolks

Cover the chiles with hot water and let soak for 15 minutes or until pliable. Drain the chiles, discarding most of the seeds. Place in a blender or food processor and puree until smooth, using a little of the soaking water if necessary. Stir in the cinnamon and cloves.

Melt the chocolate in a double boiler over hot water.

Combine the cream, milk, and sugar. Split the vanilla bean and scrape some of the seeds into the mixture. Bring to a boil.

While whisking the egg yolks, pour in about 1/3 of the hot milk mixture. Reheat the remaining milk and return the egg yolk/milk mixture to the pan. Heat for 1 minute, whisking constantly.

Strain the mixture into a bowl. Stir in the chiles and chocolate and chill.

Freeze in an ice cream maker according to the manufacturer's directions.

 Yield: 1 quart

Chiltepin Ice Cream

This novelty was first served in 1988 for the symposium on wild chiles at the Desert Botanical Garden in Phoenix and at the Fiesta de los Chiles at the Tucson Botanical Gardens. It is very hot (despite the tendency of ice cream to cut the heat), so you may want to reduce the quantity of chiltepins.

  1/3 cup chiltepines en escabeche, thoroughly rinsed, pulverized, or substitute fresh green or dried red pods
  1 gallon vanilla ice cream

Combine all ingredients and mix thoroughly in a blender until pepper flecks appear throughout the ice cream. Serve in small portions.

 Yield: 1 quart

Chile Fruit Sundae

The combination of fruit and chile is quite common in Mexico, where you can purchase fresh fruit dusted with red chile from vendors on street corners. The mix of hot and sweet provides a refreshing end to any meal.

 3 tablespoons cider vinegar
 2 tablespoons sugar
 1/4 teaspoon crushed habanero chile
 1 cup cubed watermelon
 1 cup diced fresh pineapple
 1 cup sliced fresh strawberries

Heat the vinegar and sugar until the sugar dissolves. Stir in the chile and allow to cool.

Mix the fruit together, pour the sauce over the top, and chill until serving.

Serves: 4

Cinnamon Spiced Dessert Plantains with Natilla Cream

Plantains are a staple in the Costa Rican diet, served at any meal. This recipe for dessert plantains was given to us by Melena, our Costa Rican guide to the chile plantations at Los Chiles. Bananas can be substituted if plantains are not available. The combination of sweet and sour creams is a substitute for the common table cream in Costa Rica.

 2 tablespoons butter
 1 tablespoon honey
 1/4 teaspoon ground cinnamon
 2 large plantains or bananas, peeled
    and sliced lengthwise
 3 tablespoons heavy cream
 4 tablespoons sour cream

Melt the butter and stir in the honey and cinnamon. Fry the plantains in the mixture until soft, turning once.

Combine the two creams and mix well.

Place the plantains on plates, pour some of the honey/cinnamon mixture over them, top with the cream mixture, and serve.

Serves: 2

Ibarra Chocolate Torte

In our third issue of Chile Pepper, *chef Mark Miller of the Coyote Cafe shared his creation of a torte that replaces flour with ground almonds. We have prepared this several times with great results. Mexican Ibarra chocolate can replace the bittersweet chocolate and cinnamon used here. The torte can be made up to a day in advance and should be kept at room temperature.*

2 cups unblanched almonds

Zest of 3 oranges

3 ounces bittersweet chocolate, grated

1 1/2 teaspoons ground cinnamon

6 eggs, separated and at
  room temperature

1/2 cup sugar

3 tablespoons fresh orange juice

Glaze:

5 ounces bittersweet chocolate

3 tablespoons Grand Marnier

1 tablespoon light corn syrup

3/4 cup unsalted butter

Preheat the oven to 350 degrees.

Butter bottom and sides of a 9-inch springform pan; line with parchment paper, and butter and flour the parchment paper.

Roast the almonds on a baking sheet for 5 minutes or until slightly browned. Cool. Place them in a blender or food processor and grind until fine.

Finely chop the orange zest. Combine with the roasted almonds, grated chocolate, and cinnamon.

Beat the egg yolks until light, incorporating as much air as possible. When thick, add the sugar in two parts.

In another bowl, beat the egg whites until stiff.

Beat the almond mixture, orange juice, and 1/3 of the egg whites into the egg yolks. Then rapidly fold in the remaining egg whites.

Pour the batter into the prepared pan and bake in the middle of the oven for 35 to 40 minutes, or until the cake pulls away from the sides of the pan. Loosen the sides of the pan and cool for 10 minutes. Invert onto a rack to cool; remove the paper. Cool the torte.

To make the glaze, break the chocolate into small pieces and combine all the ingredients in the top of a double boiler. Bring the water to a boil and then turn off the heat. Beat with a whisk until smooth.

Place the cake on a rack over a pan or waxed paper and pour half of the glaze in the center. Tilt the cake to distribute the glaze evenly and allow the cake to sit for 45 minutes. Repeat with remaining glaze (reheating glaze, if necessary) and let sit for 45 minutes before serving.

Serves: 10 to 12

Warm Chocolate Pecan Pie

This was one of the winners of our Great Chile Pepper Recipe Contest. Winner Stella Fong suggested: "Serve with chocolate ice cream for the ultimate chocolate experience!"

Chocolate Pie Pastry:

  1 cup unbleached flour

  2 tablespoons cocoa

  2 tablespoons sugar

  1 teaspoon ground red New Mexican chile

  2 tablespoons vegetable shortening

  1/4 cup unsalted butter

  3 tablespoons cold water

Sift all the dry ingredients together into a food processor. Add the shortening to the flour and blend. Cut the butter into chunks, add to the processor, and process until it is cut into very tiny pieces.

Add the water and continue to process until the dough wraps itself around the blade and forms a ball.

Wrap the dough in plastic and refrigerate for at least 1/2 hour. Pastry can be kept in the refrigerator for about a week or it can be frozen for several months. If frozen, defrost slowly in the refrigerator before using.

Pie Filling:

  4 tablespoons butter

  1/4 cup hot fudge sauce

  4 teaspoons ground red New Mexican chile

  3 eggs, beaten

  3/4 cup dark corn syrup

  1/2 cup dark brown sugar

  1 teaspoon vanilla

  1 1/4 cups pecan halves

Preheat the oven to 425 degrees.

Line a 9-inch pie pan with the pie pastry. Combine the butter and hot fudge and microwave on High for 1 minute.

Combine the chile, eggs, corn syrup, sugar, fudge mixture, and vanilla. Stir in the pecans and pour into the pie shell.

Bake for 15 minutes, reduce the heat to 350 degrees, and continue baking for an additional 30 minutes, or until the edges are set.

 Serves: 8 to 10

Bananas Flambé

From Jay Solomon comes this classic Caribbean dessert. "Here is the finishing touch for my cooking class on tropical cuisine," he wrote. "I conclude the class by turning down the lights, flambéing the bananas, and serving them over frozen yogurt. Everyone goes wild. I immediately hand out the instructor evaluation forms at that point, getting them while they're in a good mood!"

- 2 tablespoons butter
- 2 tablespoons brown sugar
- 4 bananas, peeled and sliced crosswise
- 1/4 teaspoon ground cinnamon
- 1/4 cup dark rum
- 1/4 cup Crème de Banana liqueur
- 1 pint vanilla or chocolate ice cream
   or frozen yogurt

Combine the butter and brown sugar in a skillet and cook over medium heat until the mixture forms a syrup, about 3 minutes.

Add the banana slices and cinnamon and saute for 3 minutes. Turn the slices to coat them thoroughly with the syrup.

Add the rum and Crème de Banana, heat briefly, and touch a match to the mixture. Allow the flame to subside and continue cooking for 1 more minute.

Scoop the ice cream into serving bowls, spoon the bananas over the ice cream, and serve.

 Serves: 4

Mango Red Chile Truffles

Kathy Redford, pastry chef of the Inn of the Anasazi in Santa Fe, created this exquisite masterpiece with an interesting chile twist.

- 1 3/4 pounds white baking chocolate, chopped into small pieces, divided
- 1 cup heavy cream
- 1 mango, chopped
- 3 teaspoons ground red
   New Mexican chile
- Ground cinnamon

Place 1 1/4 pounds of the chocolate into a bowl. Bring the cream to a rolling boil and pour over the chocolate; stir until melted. Strain the mixture and let it "set" overnight in the refrigerator. The mixture will be firm like frosting by morning.

Mix the mango and chile powder into the filling. Drop tablespoons of the filling onto a pan lined with waxed paper. Cool in the refrigerator until very firm.

Melt the remaining chocolate. Dip the chilled filling in the chocolate and let it set again in the refrigerator. Sprinkle with the cinnamon before serving.

 Yield: 24 to 30 truffles

Note: This recipe requires advance preparation.

Resources

Further Reading

Below is a listing of our favorite books concerning either hot and spicy cooking or cuisines that use chile peppers. The books are available from booksellers or libraries.

Andrews, Jean
1984. *Peppers: The Domesticated Capsicums.* Austin: University of Texas Press.
1993. *Red Hot Peppers.* New York: Macmillan.

Bhumicitr, Vatcharin
1988. *The Taste of Thailand.* Bangkok: Asia Books.

Bosland, Paul W.
1992. *Capsicum: A Comprehensive Bibliography.* Las Cruces, NM: Chile Institute.

Bridges, Bill
1994. *The Great American Chili Book.* New York: Lyons and Burford.

Brown, Bob, et al.
1971. *South American Cookbook.* New York: Dover.

Butel, Jane
1987. *Hotter than Hell.* Tucson: HP Books.

Callery, Emma, ed.
1991. *The Complete Hot and Spicy Cookbook.* Secaucus, NJ: Wellfleet Press.

Cooper, Joe
1952. *With or Without Beans.* Dallas: William S. Henson.

Cranwell, John Phillips
1975. *The Hellfire Cookbook.* New York: Quadrangle.

de Benitez, Ana M.
1974. *Pre-Hispanic Cookbook (Cocina Prehispanica).* Mexico, D.F.: Ediciones Euroamericanas Klaus Thiele.

Dent, Huntley
1985. *The Feast of Santa Fe.* New York: Simon and Schuster.

DeWitt, Dave
1991. *Hot Spots.* Rocklin, CA: Prima Publishing.
1992. *Chile Peppers: A Selected Bibliography of the Capsicums.* Las Cruces, NM: Chile Institute.

DeWitt, Dave, and Paul Bosland
1993. *The Pepper Garden.* Berkeley: Ten Speed Press.

DeWitt, Dave, and Nancy Gerlach
1984. *The Fiery Cuisines.* Berkeley: Ten Speed Press, 1991.
1986. *Fiery Appetizers.* Albuquerque: Border Books, 1991.
1990. *The Whole Chile Pepper Book.* Boston: Little, Brown & Company.
1992. *Just North of the Border.* Rocklin, CA: Prima Publishing.

DeWitt, Dave, and Arthur Pais
1994. *A World of Curries.* Boston: Little, Brown & Company.

DeWitt, Dave, and Mary Jane Wilan
1992. *The Food Lover's Handbook to the Southwest.* Rocklin, CA: Prima Publishing.
1993. *Callaloo, Calypso & Carnival: The Cuisines of Trinidad and Tobago.* Freedom, CA: Crossing Press.

DeWitt, Dave; Mary Jane Wilan; and Jeanette DeAnda
1995. *Meltdown: The Official Fiery Foods Show Cookbook and Chilehead Resource Guide.* Freedom, CA: Crossing Press.

DeWitt, Dave; Mary Jane Wilan; and Melissa T. Stock
1994. *Hot & Spicy & Meatless.* Rocklin, CA: Prima Publishing.
1994. *Hot & Spicy Chili.* Rocklin, CA: Prima Publishing.
1995. *Hot & Spicy Latin Dishes.* Rocklin, CA: Prima Publishing.

Duncan, Geraldine
1985. *Some Like It Hotter.* San Francisco: 101 Productions.

Duong, Binh, and Marcia Kiesel
1991. *Simple Art of Vietnamese Cooking.* New York: Prentice-Hall.

Gerlach, Jeffrey and Nancy
1994. *Foods of the Maya: A Taste of the Yucatan.* Freedom, CA: Crossing Press.

Halasz, Zoltan
1963. *Hungarian Paprika Through the Ages.* Budapest: Corvina Press.

Harris, Dunstan
1988. *Island Cooking: Recipes from the Caribbean.* Freedom, CA: Crossing Press.

Harris, Jessica
1985. *Hot Stuff: A Cookbook in Praise of the Piquant.* New York: Atheneum. (Also, Ballantine, 1986.)
1992. *Tasting Brazil.* New York: Macmillan.

Hatchen, Harva
1970. *Kitchen Safari.* New York: Atheneum.

Hazen-Hammon, Susan
1993. *Chile Pepper Fever: Mine's Hotter than Yours.* Stillwater, MN: Voyageur Press.

Hodgson, Moira
1977. *The Hot and Spicy Cookbook.* New York: McGraw-Hill.

Jamison, Cheryl Alters, and Bill Jamison
1991. *The Rancho de Chimayó Cookbook.* Boston: Harvard Commons Press.

Karoff, Barbara
1989. *South American Cooking.* Berkeley, CA: Aris Books.

Kennedy, Diana
1972. *The Cuisines of Mexico.* New York: Harper and Row.
1975. *The Tortilla Book.* New York: Harper and Row.
1978. *Recipes from the Regional Cooks of Mexico.* New York: Harper and Row.

Lomeli, Arturo
1986. *El Chile y Otros Picantes.* Mexico, D.F.: Asociacion Mexicana de Estudios para la Defensa del Comsumidor.

Long-Solis, Janet
1986. *Capsicum y Cultura: La Historia del Chili.* Mexico, D.F.: Fondo de Cultura Economica.

Marks, Copeland
1985. *False Tongues and Sunday Bread: A Guatemalan and Mayan Cookbook.* New York: M. Evans.
1989. *The Exotic Kitchens of Indonesia.* New York: M. Evans.

McDermott, Nancie
1992. *Real Thai.* San Francisco: Chronicle Books.

McMahan, Jacqueline
1987. *The Salsa Book.* Lake Hughes, CA: Olive Press.
1987. *Red and Green Chile Book.* Lake Hughes, CA: Olive Press.

Miller, Mark
1991. *The Great Chile Book.* Berkeley: Ten Speed Press.
1994. *The Great Salsa Book.* Berkeley: Ten Speed Press.

Murphy, Rosalea
1988. *The Pink Adobe Cookbook.* New York: Dell.

Naj, Amal
1992. *Peppers: A Story of Hot Pursuits.* New York: Knopf.

Ortiz, Elizabeth Lambert
1968. *The Complete Book of Mexican Cooking.* New York: Bantam.
1973. *The Complete Book of Caribbean Cooking.* New York: M. Evans.
1979. *The Complete Book of Latin American Cooking.* New York: Knopf.

Owen, Sri
1980. *Indonesian Food and Cookery.* London: Prospect Books.

Palazuelos, Susana, et al.
1991. *Mexico: The Beautiful Cookbook.* San Francisco: Collins.

Peyton, James W.
1990. *El Norte: The Cuisine of Northern Mexico.* Santa Fe: Red Crane Books.
1994. *La Cocina de La Frontera: Mexican-American Cooking from the Southwest.* Santa Fe: Red Crane Books.

Purseglove, J. W., et al.
1981. "Chillies: Capsicum spp." In *Spices.* London: Longman's.

Quintana, Patricia
1986. *The Taste of Mexico.* New York: Stewart, Tabori, and Chang.
1989. *Mexico's Feasts of Life.* Tulsa: Council Oak Books.

Ries, M.
1968. *The Hundred-Year History of Tabasco.* Avery Island, LA: McIlhenny Company.

Schlesinger, Chris, and John Willoughby
1990. *The Thrill of the Grill*. New York: William Morrow.
1993. *Salsas, Sambals, Chutneys and Chowchows*. New York: William Morrow.
1994. *Big Flavors of the Hot Sun*. New York: William Morrow.

Schweid, R.
1980. *Hot Peppers (Tabasco)*. Seattle: Madrona Publishing.

Solomon, Charmaine
1976. *The Complete Asian Cookbook*. New York: McGraw-Hill.

Solomon, Jay
1990. *Chutneys, Relishes & Table Sauces*. Freedom, CA: Crossing Press.
1991. *A Taste of the Tropics: Traditional and Innovative Cooking from the Pacific and Caribbean*. Freedom, CA: Crossing Press.
1994. *Global Grilling: Sizzling Recipes from Around the World*. Freedom, CA: Crossing Press.

Somos, Andras
1984. *The Paprika*. Budapest: Akademiai Kaido.

Stendahl
1979. *Spicy Food*. New York: Holt, Rinehart & Winston.

Tarantino, Jim
1992. *Marinades*. Freedom, CA: Crossing Press.

Tolbert, F. X.
1972. *A Bowl of Red*. New York: Doubleday.

Thompson, Jennifer Trainer
1994. *Hot Licks*. San Francisco: Chronicle Books.

Warren, William, et al.
1992. *Thailand: The Beautiful Cookbook*. San Francisco: Collins.

Willinsky, Helen
1990. *Jerk: Barbecue from Jamaica*. Freedom, CA: Crossing Press.

Wolfe, Linda
1970. *The Cooking of the Caribbean Islands*. New York: Time-Life Books.

Mail-Order Catalogs

These are the main mail-order suppliers of the hot and spicy products called for in this cookbook.

Blazing Chile Bros.
(800) 473-9040

Calido Chile Traders
5360 Merriam Drive
Merriam, KS 66203
(800) 568-8468

Chile Pepper Magazine
P.O. Box 80780
Albuquerque, NM 87198
(800) 359-1483

Chile Today, Hot Tamale
919 Highway 33, Suite 47
Freehold, NJ 07728
(800) 468-7377

Colorado Spice Company
5030 Nome Street, Unit A
Denver, CO 80239
(800) 67-SPICE

Coyote Cocina
1364 Rufina Circle #1
Santa Fe, NM 87501
(800) 866-HOWL

Dean and DeLuca
Mail Order Department
560 Broadway
New York, NY 10012
(212) 431-1691

Don Alfonso Foods
P.O. Box 201988
Austin, TX 78720
(800) 456-6100

Enchanted Seeds
P.O. Box 6087
Las Cruces, NM 88006
(505) 233-3033

Flamingo Flats
Box 441
St. Michael's, MD 21663
(800) 468-8841

Frieda's, Inc.
P.O. Box 584888
Los Angeles, CA 90058
(800) 421-9477

GMB Specialty Foods, Inc.
Norma Bishop Mustard & Sauces
Scottsdale Mustard Co.
Gourmet Mustard Co.
P.O. Box 962
San Juan Capistrano, CA 92693-0962
(714) 240-3053

Gourmet Gallery
320 North Highway 89A
Singua Plaza
Sedona, AZ 86336
(800) 888-3484

Hell's Kitchen Inc.
216 Lippincott Avenue
Riverside, NJ 08075
(609) 764-1487

Hot Sauce Club of America
P.O. Box 687
Indian Rocks Beach
FL 34635-0687
(800) SAUCE-2-U

Hot Sauce Harry's
The Dallas Farmer's Market
3422 Flair Drive
Dallas, Texas 75229
(214) 902-8552

Le Saucier
Faneuil Hall Marketplace
Boston, MA 02109
(617) 227-9649

Lotta Hotta
3150 Mercier, Suite 516
Kansas City, MO 64111
(816) 931-6700

Melissa's World Variety Produce
P.O. Box 21127
Los Angeles, CA 90021
(800) 468-7111

Nancy's Specialty Market
P.O. Box 327
Wye Mills, MD 21679
(800) 462-6291

Old Southwest Trading Company
P.O. Box 7545
Albuquerque, NM 87194
(505) 836-0168

Pendery's
304 East Belknap
Fort Worth, TX 76102
(800) 533-1879

The Pepper Gal
P.O. Box 23006
Ft. Lauderdale, FL 33307
(305) 537-5540

Pepper Joe's, Inc.
7 Tyburn Court
Timonium, MD 21093
(410) 561-8158

Santa Fe School of Cooking
116 W. San Francisco Street
Santa Fe, NM 87501
(505) 983-4511

Shepherd's Garden Seeds
6116 Highway 9
Felton, CA 95018
(408) 335-6910

South Side Pepper Co.
320 N. Walnut Street
Mechanicsburg, PA 17055
(717) 691-7132

Retail Shops

Listed below are retail shops or markets that specialize in hot and spicy products. Some of them have mail-order catalogs. It has been difficult to keep up with the explosion in hot shop retailers, so we apologize if we have missed any. For shops listed with post office boxes, call first for directions to their locations.

Calido Chile Traders
5360 Merriam Drive
Merriam, KS 66203
(913) 384-0019; (800) 568-8468

Caribbean Spice Company
2 South Church Street
Fairhope, AL 36532
(800) 990-6088

Central Market
4001 North Lamar
Austin, TX 78756
(512) 206-1000

Chile Hill Emporium
Box 9100
Bernalillo, NM 87004
(505) 867-3294

The Chile Shop
109 East Water Street
Santa Fe, NM 87501
(505) 983-6080

Chili Patch U.S.A.
204 San Felipe N.W.
Albuquerque, NM 87104
(505) 242-4454; (800) 458-0646

Chili Pepper Emporium
328 San Felipe N.W.
Albuquerque, NM 87104
(505) 242-7538

Chili Pepper Mania
1709-F Airline Hwy., P.O. Box 232
Hollister, CA 95023
(408) 636-8259

Chutneys
143 Delaware Street
Lexington, OH 44904
(419) 884-2853

Colorado Spice Company
5030 Nome Street, Unit A
Denver, CO 80239
(303) 373-0141; (800) 67-SPICE

Coyote Cafe General Store
132 West Water Street
Santa Fe, NM 87501
(505) 982-2454; (800) 866-HOWL

Dat'l Do-It Hot Shop
P.O. Box 4019
St. Augustine, FL 32085
(904) 824-5303; (800) HOT-DATL

Dat'l Do-It Hot Shop
Dadeland Mall
7535 North Kendall Drive
Miami, FL 37211
(305) 253-0248

Down Island Ventures
P.O. Box 37
Cruz Bay
St. John, U.S. Virgin Islands 00832
(809) 693-7200

Eagle Mountain Gifts
634 South China Lake Boulevard
Ridgecrest, CA 93555
(619) 375-3071

Fiery Foods
909 20th Avenue South
Nashville, TN 37212
(615) 320-5475

Free Spirit
420 South Mill Avenue
Tempe, AZ 85281
(602) 966-4339

Gourmet Gallery
320 North Highway 89A
Singua Plaza
Sedona, AZ 86336
(520) 282-2682

Garden Gate Gift Shop
Tucson Botanical Gardens
2150 North Alvernon Way
Tucson, AZ 85712
(602) 326-9686

GMB Specialty Foods, Inc.
P.O. Box 962
San Juan Capistrano, CA 92693-0962
(714) 240-3053

Hatch Chile Express
P.O. Box 350
Hatch, NM 87937
(505) 267-3226

Hell's Kitchen Inc.
Route 130 at Route 73
Haddonfield Road
Pennsauken, NJ 08010
(609) 663-6666

Hot Hot Hot
56 South Delacey Avenue
Pasadena, CA 91105
(818) 564-1090; (800) 959-7742
e-mail hothothot@ Earthlink.net
URL http://www.hot.presence.com/hot/

Hot Kicks
4349 Raymir Place
Wauwatosa, WI 53222
(414) 536-7808

Hot Licks
P.O. Box 7854
Hollywood, FL 33081
(305) 987-7105

Hot Lovers Fiery Foods
1282 Wolseley Avenue
Winnipeg, Manitoba R3G 1H4
Canada
(204) 772-6418

Hot Papa's Fiery Flavors
11121 Weeden Road
Randolph, NY 14772
(716) 358-4302

The Hot Spot
5777 South Lakeshore Drive
Shreveport, LA 71119
(318) 635-3581

The Hot Spot
1 Riverfront Plaza #300
Lawrence, KS 66044
(913) 841-7200

Hot Stuff
288 Argonne Avenue
Long Beach, CA 90803
(310) 438-1118

Hot Stuff
227 Sullivan Street
New York, NY 10012
(212) 254-6120; (800) 466-8206

Hots for You—
Chili Pepper Emporium
8843 Shady Meadow Drive
Sandy, UT 84093
(801) 255-7800

Jones and Bones
621 Capitola Avenue
Capitola, CA 95010
(408) 462-0521

Le Saucier
Faneuil Hall Marketplace
Boston, MA 02109
(617) 227-9649

Lotta Hotta
3150 Mercier, Suite 516
Kansas City, MO 64111
(816) 931-6700

The Original Hot Sauce Company
Avenue of Shops
1421-C Larimer Street
Denver, CO 80202
(303) 615-5812

**New Orleans
School of Cooking**
620 Decatur Street
New Orleans, LA 70130
(504) 482-3632

Pampered Pirate
4 Norre Gade
St. Thomas, U.S. Virgin Islands 00802
(809) 775-5450
Mailing address: P.O. Box 590
St. Thomas, U.S. Virgin Islands 00804

Peppers
2009 Highway 1
Dewey Beach, DE 19971
(302) 227-1958; (800) 998-3473

Pepperhead Hot Shoppe
7036 Kristi Court
Garner, NC 27529
(919) 553-4576

Pepper Joe's, Inc.
7 Tyburn Court
Timonium, MD 21093
(410) 561-8158

Potpourri
303 Romero NW
Plaza Don Luis, Old Town
Albuquerque, NM 87104
(505) 243-4087

Pungent Pod
25 Haviland Road
Queensbury, NY 12804
(518) 793-3180

Rivera's Chile Shop
109 1/2 Concho Street
San Antonio, TX 78207
(210) 226-9106

Salsas, Etc.!
3683 Tunis Avenue
San Jose, CA 95132
(408) 263-6392

Salsas, Etc.!
374 Eastridge Mall
San Jose, CA 95122
(408) 223-9020

Sambet's Cajun Store
8644 Spicewood Springs Road, Suite F
Austin, TX 78759
(800) 472-6238

Santa Fe Emporium
104 West San Francisco Street
Santa Fe, NM 87501
(505) 984-1966

Santa Fe School of Cooking
116 West San Francisco Street
Santa Fe, NM 87501
(505) 983-4511

Santa Fe Trading Company
7 Main Street
Tarrytown, NY 10591
(914) 332-1730

Señor Chile's at Rawhide
23020 North Scottsdale Road
Scottsdale, AZ 85255
(602) 563-5600

Sherwood's Lotsa Hotsa
P.O. Box 2106
Lakeside, CA 92040
(619) 443-7982

Some Like It Hot
3208 Scott Street
San Francisco, CA 94123
(415) 441-7HOT

Some Like It Hot
301 South Light Street
Harbor Place
Baltimore, MD 21202
(410) 547-2HOT

A Southern Season
Eastgate Shopping Center
P.O. Box 2678
Chapel Hill, NC 27515
(800) 253-3663

The Stonewall
Chili Pepper Company
P.O. Box 241
Stonewall, TX 78671
(210) 644-2667; (800) 232-2995

Sunbelt Shows
P.O. Box 4980
Albuquerque, NM 87196
(505) 873-9103

Sunny Caribbee Spice Company
P.O. Box 3237
St. Thomas, U.S. Virgin Islands 00803
(809) 494-2178

Tabasco Country Store
Avery Island, LA 70513
(318) 365-8173

Tabasco Country Store
Riverwalk Marketplace
1 Poydras Street
New Orleans, LA 70130
(504) 523-1711

Uncle Bill's House of Hot Sauce
311 North Higgins Avenue
Missoula, MT 59801
(406) 543-5627

The Whole Earth Grainery
111 Ivinson Avenue
Laramie, WY 82070
(307) 745-4268

Seed Companies

Looking to grow your own? These companies carry a wide selection of chile pepper seed varieties.

The Cook's Garden
P.O. Box 535
Londonderry, VT 05148
(802) 824-3400

Enchanted Seeds
P.O. Box 6087
Las Cruces, NM 88006
(505) 233-3033

Native Seeds / SEARCH
2509 Campbell Avenue #325
Tucson, AZ 85719

Old Southwest Trading Company
P.O. Box 7545
Albuquerque, NM 87194
(505) 836-0168

The Pepper Gal
P.O. Box 12534
Lake Park, FL 33403
(305) 537-5540

Plants of the Southwest
Agua Fria Route 6, Box 11A
Santa Fe, NM 87501
(505) 438-8888

Redwood City Seed Co.
P.O. Box 361
Redwood City, CA 94064
(415) 325-SEED

Seed Savers Exchange
Route 3, Box 239
Decorah, IA 52101

Seeds of Change
1364 Rufina Circle #5
Santa Fe, NM 87501
(505) 983-8956

Seeds West
P.O. Box 1739
El Prado, NM 87529
(505) 758-7268

Shepherd's Garden Seeds
6116 Highway 9
Felton, CA 95018
(408) 335-6910

Twilley Seed Co.
P.O. Box 65
Trevose, PA 19053
(800) 622-SEED

Index

About the Editors

Dave DeWitt is one of the foremost authorities in the world on chile peppers and spicy foods. He is the editor of *Chile Pepper* Magazine, and co-author of *Meltdown: The Official Fiery Foods Show Cookbook and Chilehead Resource Guide, The Fiery Cuisines, The Whole Chile Pepper Book* and *Callaloo, Calypso and Carnival: The Cuisines of Trinidad and Tobago*. He is the co-producer of the National Fiery Foods Show and lives in Albuquerque.

Nancy Gerlach, a registered dietician, currently serves as Food Editor of *Chile Pepper* Magazine. She is the co-author of *The Fiery Cuisines, Fiery Appetizers, Just North of the Border, The Whole Chile Pepper Book,* and *Foods of the Maya*. She lives in Albuquerque with her husband Jeffrey where they operate The Old Southwest Trading Company, a wholesale and mail-order chile company.

Notes

Notes

Notes

Notes

Notes

The Crossing Press

publishes a full selection of

cookbooks. To receive our

current catalog,

please call toll-free,

800-777-1048.